Influential Women

Influential Women

From the New
Testament to today –
how women can build
up (or undermine)
their local church

WENDY VIRGO

MONARCH
BOOKS
Oxford, UK & Grand Rapids, Michigan, USA

First published in the UK in 2009 by Monarch Books
(a publishing imprint of Lion Hudson plc),
Wilkinson House, Jordan Hill Road, Oxford OX2 8DR.
Tel: +44 (0)1865 302750 Fax: +44 (0)1865 302757
Email: monarch@lionhudson.com
www.lionhudson.com

ISBN: 978-1-85424-921-0 (UK)
ISBN: 978-0-8254-6320-4 (USA)

Distributed by:
UK: Marston Book Services Ltd, PO Box 269, Abingdon, Oxon OX14 4YN;
USA: Kregel Publications, PO Box 2607, Grand Rapids, Michigan 49501

This book has been printed on paper and board independently certified as having come from sustainable forests.

British Library Cataloguing Data
A catalogue record for this book is available from the British Library.

Printed and bound in England by CPI Cox & Wyman.

CONTENTS

Acknowledgements

To my daughter Anna, and my daughters-in-law, Rachel, Kate, Caroline and Esme – all beautiful, influential Christian women.

My grateful thanks to Susan Brooks and Ruth Brading of Grace City Church, Sydney, Australia, for their helpful comments and advice.

To all the wonderful women in Newfrontiers churches all over the world who are influencing their churches, impacting their cultures and helping to change the world.

Foreword

One of the remarkable things about the Bible that often surprises newcomers to it is the fact that it is full of real-life stories about flesh-and-blood people just like us. Some of them may legitimately be called "saints", but even they did not walk nine inches off the ground, sport glowing haloes around their heads, or sprout wings from between their shoulder blades! Instead, they endured very hard times, faced enormous temptations, and coped with overwhelming challenges that would crush and break many of us today.

Just about everybody loves a good story. We seem to be insatiably hungry for them, especially when they involve characters we find interesting and real, whose lives are full of drama and surprise. Stories grip, move, warn us against error and inspire us to achieve great things. The Bible contains some of the best and most memorable in the world. Judging by the demand we see everywhere for films, drama series, television soap-operas, plays, best-selling novels, celebrity gossip and well-written biographies, it seems we cannot get enough of such stories, and God knew this too. So in the Bible, he has given us some of the best stories ever written, but with this difference: they all happen to be true. God gave them to us because they are pictorial to enable us to picture their characters vividly, concrete so that we can connect with them meaningfully, and unforgettable to help burn their lessons into our memories, until they eventually transform our thinking and behaviour by the power of the Holy Spirit who was there when all these events happened.

Tragically, most of the stories we read, watch, or hear about today, are degrading and depressing. We live in a culture that is entertained by lust, unfaithfulness, rebellion, murder, sadistic cruelty, broken relationships, disintegration and death, as if that was all there is to life. These things happen, of course, but this isn't life as God intended it to be or how he is willing to empower us to experience it differently. This is why the Bible tells it like it is, but also opens up to us new possibilities for redemptive life and positive change in our lives. Its stories do not trade on an unbroken diet of "bottom-up" despair, but rather a "top-down" promise of hope from God that offers us viable alternatives to the widespread mood of futility and pointlessness we see all around us today.

Every woman is unique and no two are the same. Wendy Virgo explores this fact to the full. She knows that all women have a special calling from God, and that there are all kinds of ways women may pursue the greatness God has ordained for them in Christ. Wendy addresses a fascinating selection of biblical heroines and villains, many of whom discovered God's best for them while others failed badly due to the pull of seductive but destructive alternatives. Wendy is a stand-out woman of God herself, with a remarkable ministry to women. It's wonderful that she here shares so freely some of the greatest things the Lord has taught her so that others can discover them too, offering a wealth of practical and theological wisdom that will help many to become outstanding women of God themselves.

With profound insight and total honesty about her own past failures and personal breakthroughs, Wendy explores "the good, the bad, and the ugly" of Bible women. Here are great role models, real "minxes" and rich ministries, whose timeless stories help us to enter the gritty reality of their lives. We're then treated to some of the most astonishingly helpful insights and relevant theology that I have read anywhere. Wendy is not afraid to voice strong opinions about some of the most controversial issues of the hour concerning the dignity, equality, anointing, role relationships, complementary gifts and God-given importance of women in the church today. I think that just as I did, you will find *Influential Women* to be one of the best Bible character books you have ever read.

Greg Haslam
Minister, Westminster Chapel, London

Introduction

When I was growing up, young women who had applied to the Overseas Missionary Fellowship, formerly the China Inland Mission, often used to come and stay with our family for the weekend. My mother was on the committee which interviewed these prospective young missionaries and part of the selection process was that they should come individually to stay with us for a weekend, during which time my mother would have long conversations with them and observe them in different situations.

Two of these young women stand out in my memory because they were so different from the rest: they were vivacious, pretty and fun. One was very sporty and gave me her tennis racquet before she left. The other was an attractive German girl. I remember being at a weekend conference party, where she seemed to be constantly surrounded by young men! The other candidates blur into a hazy picture of terrible, frumpy clothes, and earnest, scrubbed faces innocent of make-up, under unstyled hair randomly gathered into wispy "buns" from which hairpins threatened to escape. To me they were boring, and I did not want to be like them! But they seemed to constitute in my mind a stereotype of Christian women, especially women who were called to radical service. This was sad because I definitely wanted to be "called".

(I feel somewhat ashamed now of my superficial assessment. I have read books about women missionaries in China which chronicle their breathtaking achievements: women like the intrepid trio, Evangeline and Francesca

French, and Mildred Cable, who travelled extensively in virtually uncharted territory through northwest China and the Gobi Desert. They travelled by donkey, ox cart and on foot in extreme temperatures, staying at primitive inns, in an era when women were expected to stay at home and knit. Susie Garland was another highly educated, refined young lady who spent most of her life in China and invented a script which vastly simplified reading, enabling hitherto illiterate Chinese women to learn to read. These women and many others laid down their lives to open up interior China and bring the gospel to thousands of people. I would not want to diminish their amazing achievements. I was obviously very immature when I met the young candidates whom my mother was interviewing.)

My family belonged to the local Brethren assembly, a fact which did nothing to dispel the gloomy picture. All the women were required to wear hats as a symbol of submission, but were not allowed to utter a word in church meetings. They more than made up for this at home, of course! The meetings themselves were not very inspiring and I spent many Sunday mornings watching the clock tick slowly round to midday. As a child, I found some escape when I learned to read, because the long silences afforded plenty of opportunity to delve into the mysteries of the books of the Bible. Revelation was particularly fascinating with its beasts and dragons; the Song of Songs was pretty and poetic, but any meaning totally eluded me. Of course the hats worn by the women were a source of interest; eventually, as I became a baptized member, I had to wear one myself.

As a teenager, I swung between wanting to be a thoroughgoing, authentic Christian who would toe the line, and rebelling against what I perceived as the petty constraints placed on Christian women. I wanted to be pretty, wear make-up, go on dates, go to the cinema, but any girl who did such things was considered to be shallow and not "keen". Christians only began to go to the cinema when *Mary Poppins* and *The Sound of Music* came to our screens, films which were deemed harmless enough not to be a corrupting influence! The result was that I and most of my friends did it all, but secretly. I had a little cache of make-up which I took along to parties and applied when I arrived. Dates were usually furtively accomplished.

However, in later years, as I began to explore the Bible for myself, I found that there were no stereotypes of women in its pages. I was relieved to discover that in the New Testament church we can find rich and poor, old and young, mothers and grandmothers, career women and prophetesses. I read of Priscilla, a refugee who traipsed around the Mediterranean with her husband Aquila, and of Tabitha, a woman whose needlework skill was so indispensable to the church that when she died an apostle was sent for, to raise her from the dead!

I found that women can be powerful forces in a church and can be influential in changing it from a healthy community to a sick one, or *vice versa*. They can be a tremendous asset or a huge liability. Whether single or married, career women or homemakers, or both, they can influence the whole ambience of a church. They can inspire the next generation or cause sourness and cynicism. We can learn from the pitfalls of the early church and so avoid similar mistakes, and we can be encouraged by the fine examples of some of the first female converts, such as Lydia and Priscilla. The pages of the New Testament contain a surprising number of references to women to whom we can relate, as we seek to build good, healthy churches in the 21st century.

While we rejoice in the diversity of women both in the early church and in our own times, it is important to remember that there are principles spelled out in the New Testament which must be the guidelines of all our behaviour. These principles are appropriate to all Christian women, whichever century they were born in, but before we discuss them we need to know the basic doctrines of our faith. These represent more than just the ground of our assurance (of forgiveness, salvation, sanctification and ultimate glorification); in other words, they are not abstract truths. They also have a huge bearing on how we live. I am increasingly persuaded that the more we know and understand about God himself (his purity, majesty and power, his love and mercy, the relationships in the Trinity) and the more we understand ourselves as human beings (the heights from which we have fallen, the implications of the cross, and the plan of God to reclaim us and use us to reveal something of himself to the world), the more motivated we become to live as God desires us to live.

CHAPTER 1

Two Quarrelling Women

I plead with Euodia and I plead with Syntyche to agree with each other in the Lord. Yes, and I ask you, loyal yoke-fellow, help these women who have contended at my side in the cause of the gospel, along with Clement and the rest of my fellow-workers whose names are in the book of life.

PHILIPPIANS 4:2–3

Euodia was chatting in a corner with Clement's wife. It was still early on Sunday morning and the heat had not yet penetrated the cool courtyard. Vine leaves were curling over trellis work, and water trickled into an ornamental pool. It would be hot later on, but Lydia's spacious house was a pleasant refuge for the saints to meet in. They were gathering now on this first day of the week. Some of the men were helping to put out chairs, and many of the women were arriving with covered baskets containing food to be shared later at the "love feast", the meal with which they ended their meetings.

Euodia glanced around, and a frown creased her forehead. She deliberately turned her back and gazed fixedly away from the doorway. Clement's wife turned to see what had prompted this behaviour; it was as she suspected: Syntyche had come in. Her heart sank as she watched an angry flush spread over Syntyche's face and neck. The woman's mouth set into a hard line as she flounced over to the opposite side of the courtyard.

Clement's wife sighed. This was getting ridiculous! The trouble was that neither of the women would yield, and now others were getting drawn into their feud. It had started over such a trivial matter, something that really was unimportant. Yet the church they all belonged to was composed of an amazingly disparate group of people who had learned to love one another, despite enormous differences.

Take Lydia, for example: a wealthy businesswoman from Thyatira across the Aegean Sea. After her husband died she had taken on his business, dealing in purple dye, a hugely expensive commodity extracted from a tiny shellfish. Only wealthy people, such as the Roman aristocracy, could afford to dress in cloth dyed in this way. Thyatira was a centre for this industry, and Lydia's family became very wealthy. She proved to be extremely able in running the business, and was able to buy another house in Philippi as well as her home in Thyatira.

But although she was successful, Lydia's heart was empty. Searching for truth, she had decided to investigate Judaism and began to meet with a group of Jewish women down by the river. Then one day, Paul had turned up with three friends, and as they preached their message, Lydia's heart was opened to receive the gospel!

Then there was the little slave girl, rescued from the abusive clutches of a couple of men. They had exploited her apparent gift of fortune-telling, taking every penny for themselves, and keeping her in abject slavery and poverty.

She had had no self-respect, no identity, no possessions, but she was set free, saved and added to the growing group of believers.

Perhaps even more striking was the conversion of the Roman jailer and his family. After the slave girl was delivered of the evil spirit that was driving her, her owners, deprived of an easy income, had seized Paul and Silas and dragged them before the authorities, accusing them of insurrection. Paul and Silas were thrown into jail. During the night, a violent earthquake shook the prison, and all the cell doors burst open! The jailer, in despair, was about to end his life, when Paul forestalled him. True to form, Paul seized the opportunity to preach the gospel to him, with the result that the man and his household were saved and added to the church.

***

We see that this church at Philippi was made up of a hugely diverse group of people: Jews, Greeks and Romans, men and women, rich and poor, members of the upper class and freed slaves. Yet they were all united by their love for Jesus and by joy in their salvation. There were so many issues that could have resulted in long-term division, but they were learning to forbear, forgive, love and serve one another.

What had happened to spoil this happy situation?

People are always looking for a perfect church; the joke is, of course, that as soon as they find one and join it, it is no longer perfect! Every church is at risk of division, and often it is through secondary issues that conflict arises. What do we know of these two unfortunate women, Euodia and Syntyche?

Hard-working, loyal Christians

First of all, they were hard-working, loyal Christian women. They were not evil! They were not masquerading as Christians; they had not infiltrated the church under false pretences. Paul does not dismiss them, pour withering scorn on them, or belittle their achievements. In fact he speaks warmly, commending them. Their names, he says, are in the book of life! This implies that they have been accepted by God, and he is not about to throw them out of his church for spoiling it. No, Paul gives them due dignity as fellow-Christians.

He also goes on to commend Euodia and Syntyche as those who have "contended at my side in the cause of the gospel", along with other fellow-workers. How many people could own that distinction? To have actually worked alongside the apostle was not something that everyone could claim. One wonders what it entailed. Doubtless, these two women had to make difficult decisions when adhering to Christian values in a pagan society. Perhaps they were despised and slandered. They may have been part of an evangelistic team, even taking their turn in giving testimony and preaching the gospel. The use of the word "contended" implies that they were at times involved in conflict, but they evidently stood firm and did not back off from their convictions. They were courageous, loyal and unswerving.

We need to see that Paul does not allow the current

behaviour of these women to sour his attitude to them, or to the undoubtedly good things they had accomplished. He affirms them. Too often, when people are not walking in step with others, they cast shadows on past history, speaking derogatively of actions and achievements which actually have been fruitful and positive.

The issue was not the issue!

So what was the dispute between these two women all about? Paul does not go into detail. In fact, for him, the issue is not the issue. He is not interested in their argument, only in the health of the church which is being threatened by the tense, edgy atmosphere produced by these quarrelling women. He does not take sides. He does not wish to enter into discussion about who is right and who is wrong; he is simply anxious for them to reconcile – and quickly!

The fact that Paul does not enter into the dispute persuades me that it was most probably over a trivial matter. If, for example, one of the women had been flirting with, or sleeping with, the other's husband, that would have been a moral issue requiring a stringent disciplinary process in which the church elders would have been involved.

Could it have been a doctrinal disagreement? Maybe, but I tend to think that, if one or both of the women had been vocal in challenging foundational doctrine or in seeking to propagate error, then again Paul would have been exact and focused in isolating the problem and instructing elders to deal with it. This would not have been alluded to vaguely in two verses. Here the apostle puts the responsibility back on the women to sort it out, not on the eldership.

Potential pitfalls

So what kinds of things cause women to disagree? There are so many potential pitfalls. In that racially mixed church, perhaps one woman was Greek and the other Jewish, provoking cultural problems (their names, however, suggest that they were both of Greek origin). Certainly, cultural issues will undoubtedly continue to raise their heads today as we seek to build multiracial churches, and we must guard against these becoming divisive.

Both Euodia and Syntyche seem to have been involved in ministry of some kind. Perhaps jealousy reared its ugly head. Perhaps one felt she was being ignored while the other was gaining recognition. Perhaps Syntyche was given to prophesying, and her prophecies were highly regarded, while Euodia had occasional prophecies but did not really flow fluently in the gift, causing her disappointment and aggravation. Surely not, we might say! But in all honesty, have not many Christian woman heard another woman share a testimony or word of encouragement, and wished they had stepped out in faith themselves? I have felt this way ... and I have had to repent of jealousy, a very destructive force if allowed to fester.

Close on the heels of jealousy is competitiveness. This is where wrong motivation confuses the picture. We are exhorted to seek spiritual gifts, but for the right reasons. They are intended to edify the church, to build everyone up, not to bolster a person's own ego. The only things we should be seeking to outdo one another in are expressions of love, such as serving one another, forgiving one another, and loving one another.

Other things that can divide women are thoughtless behaviour, criticism and selfishness. The glory of the church is that we have been saved out of a myriad of different backgrounds, and are all sinners who have been redeemed but not yet fully sanctified. Those who have been Christians for a long time must give grace to the "babes in Christ", while the new converts need to give respect to the more mature in Christ.

This, of course, leads on to another potential source of discord: personality clashes. The extrovert bounces into her house-group with a story of how she has witnessed to someone in the checkout queue at the supermarket; her kids are loud and noisy like her, and wherever she goes, tranquillity is disrupted. She hardly notices the quiet little woman who always sits by the window, but when she does, she seems tolerantly amused by her boring life. Meanwhile, the quiet little woman has just come from a long day working in a hospice, where she sat with a patient who died only two hours ago. She is longing to be replenished in God's presence and wishes the loud young mother would just be quiet!

Women may also be divided by their differing views on raising families, spending money and on styles of dress. This can be tricky: younger Christians sometimes need the guidance of older women in all of these areas, and others too. An older woman may need to help a younger woman to adapt her style of clothing to be more modest and less provocative for the sake of the men in the church. She must be careful, however, that her eagerness to help is not motivated by personal preference but by the word of God. The basic criterion must be, "Is this style modest?" This may lead to some interesting discussion of what "modesty" implies. The older woman must tactfully lead her young friend to understand that "modest" doesn't mean "frumpy and out of date"; but it does demand that hemlines and necklines don't expose so much flesh that they give problems to the men around them.

A church I knew years ago nearly came to grief when an elder's wife insisted that the girls should not wear earrings! Actually, this was potentially more serious than one might suppose, because lurking underneath was a legalistic mindset that had not yet understood the grace of God. The earring issue was a symptom of something deeply embedded which eventually had to be dealt with very deliberately. Wearing or not wearing earrings is immaterial: a girl is at liberty to wear earrings or not. What must be clear is that holiness is not built on adherence to rules about external issues; it is about attitudes of the heart, set against the prevailing mindset of the world which is implacably opposed to the purity of behaviour, motive and affections in which God delights.

Lack of forgiveness is another submerged rock on which church unity can founder. When past history and disagreements are not allowed to rest, but are continually referred to, or used as an excuse to put down another person, peace and unity will not grow.

If there is one thing which all Christians must excel at, it is forgiveness. "Be kind to one another, tender-hearted, forgiving each other, just as God in Christ also has forgiven you" (Ephesians 4:32).

All these things: jealousy and competitiveness, a judgemental attitude, legalism, hypocrisy, selfish and immature behaviour, personality clashes, different priorities, and lack of forgiveness can all be causes of disagreement. Sadly, it is often some small incident, escalating into an enormous row, which divides a church. I once heard of a church which divided because a woman had brought in an electric kettle for use at some church event. Then someone else borrowed it and a dispute arose. Husbands took sides, and others became embroiled. Neither side would give way and eventually pride, rigidity and selfishness split the church.

So what can we do if a dispute arises between women?

How did Paul address this dispute?

First, he directly addressed both women by name. There was no pussyfooting around! It was, in effect, a command: "You women, get together, and get over it – quickly! No arguing! You can do this." He was robustly confrontational.

His appeal was that they should agree with each other "in the Lord". They were both Christians. Their standing was equal before God: forgiven sinners, washed in his blood, saved by grace. Like them, we have no special rights or reason for superiority. Elsewhere, Paul says we are to be reconciled to one another because we have been "reconciled to God" (2 Corinthians 5:20). Reconciliation is at the heart of the gospel. It requires humility, putting aside personal preferences, and being aware and motivated by the health of the whole body. It is also being aware that the church needs to present to the world a community of peace, love and forgiveness. How the world loves to expose a church in conflict!

Notice that Paul also urged the two women "to agree"; some other translations, such as the King James Version, render this as: "be of the same mind", which is really more emphatic. Must we all think the same, then? Is there no room for personal preferences, taste or opinions?

The church is certainly not intended to be a bunch of clones, all living and thinking uniformly. Its very diversity is part of its glory! Yet, earlier in the epistle, Paul has urged, "[Stand] firm in one spirit, with one mind striving together for the faith of the gospel" (Philippians 1:27). Then again:

> *Make my joy complete by being of the same mind, maintaining the same love, united in spirit, intent on one purpose. Do nothing from selfishness or empty conceit, but with humility of mind regard one another as more important than yourselves; do not merely look out for your own personal interests, but also for the interests of others.*
>
> PHILIPPIANS 2:2–4

In other words, no one should be sticking out for his or her rights, or imposing his or her ideas or preferences on any others. Our motivation must be a sincere desire for the good of the whole. On primary issues (such as doctrinal and moral issues) we must take care to be of one heart, while giving grace to one another in secondary issues (such as length of hair, whether women should wear make-up, and leisure pursuits).

In appealing directly to the two women, Paul is effectively saying, "This is your responsibility." He is direct; but he is also respectful and tender, commending them, as we have seen.

He also suggests turning to a third party to help. In fact, he asks someone called Syzygus to intervene. (Syzygus actually means "yoke-fellow", so Paul may have been appealing to the church leader to step in and share the load, not just to a man of that name.) In dealing with any dispute it is important to gain a clear sense of perspective and get things in proportion, and a third party can be very helpful in doing just that. A respected friend could be called upon to fulfil this role, or a cell leader, elder, or pastor's wife, as long as the person chosen can be trusted to be impartial.

Some commentators have suggested that the whole of the epistle to the church at Philippi was written because of the dispute between Euodia and Syntyche, and that all the sublime doctrine and revelation of the previous chapters were leading up to this point. In fact, however, many of the epistles are written in this way: a systematic unfolding of doctrine followed by intensely practical instructions for working out its implications in daily life. Paul is saying, in effect, "In view of these things, this is how you ought to live."

The unity of the body of Christ is vital and anything that threatens the health of the local church must be dealt with thoroughly and ruthlessly. The miracle of the church is that it is a community of people who, apart from Christ, would not have found one another, let alone be enabled to live together in love. Grumbling and moaning, criticism and slander must not find air space among us because they affect the climate of love and acceptance which must prevail. If that climate does not prevail, then we are no different from any other community with its squabbles, feuds, gossip and backstabbing. Fallen human nature makes it impossible for human beings to live in perpetual harmony if they have not been transformed by the gospel and by their recognition of Jesus as Lord.

Years ago, when Terry and I were involved in planting our first church, I developed a wrong attitude towards another woman. It was mostly irritation on my part; I considered her children to be annoying and badly behaved, and felt that she was not disciplining them properly. I myself did not yet have any children, a fact which shows how well qualified I was to make any sort of judgement on the subject – not qualified at all! But I allowed my bad attitude towards this young mother to fester until I realized it was having a serious effect on my own walk with God. I had even begun to pray that she and her family would leave the town! Things came to a head one Sunday when we were taking communion and I felt convicted as we were exhorted to examine ourselves.

That night when it was bedtime I said to Terry, "You go up to bed, I need to pray. I'll come up later." So I knelt down by the side of a chair to pray. For some reason, I decided to write down all the things I disliked about the other woman. When I was finished, I sat back on my heels and read through my list, satisfied that it contained good reasons for disliking anyone, and that I was fairly justified in my position! Then something happened that completely shattered me. God spoke very clearly. He said, "You have just written down a picture of yourself." I was broken. How could I hold a self-righteous, condemning attitude to anyone when I was so unpleasant myself? Before God, I acknowledged that the "log" in my eye was so gross that it completely obliterated the "speck" in the other person's eye (see Matthew 7:3–5).

A few days later, the woman came to see me and we had a very uncomfortable evening together, during which we confessed to each other the reasons why we did not get on. We ended by agreeing to work at our relationship. From then on, we began to see each other, not necessarily to talk about areas of dispute, but just to make friends. I suddenly realized about six months later that if she and her family were to leave, it would break my heart! God had done something new in both of us. Sometimes I wonder what would have happened if God had not stepped in and changed my heart.

God is gracious. He knows our weaknesses, yet does not condemn us. But we cannot stay as we are! We must be changed if we are to build healthy, mature churches.

Questions for group discussion

- **How would you differentiate between primary issues and secondary issues?**
- **How should we behave toward those with whom we disagree?**
- **How do you respond to correction?**
- **What issues can divide women?**

CHAPTER 2

Women Discipling Women

Older women ... are to be reverent in their behaviour, not malicious gossips nor enslaved to much wine, teaching what is good, so that they can encourage the young women to love their husbands, to love their children, to be sensible, pure, workers at home, kind, being subject to their own husbands, so that the word of God will not be dishonoured.

Titus 2:3–5

Chloe heaved her bulky frame up and ambled off down the dusty road, blinking in the strong afternoon sun. Her mind was somewhat hazy; she had slept longer than she had intended after her midday meal, which had included an ample amount of Sicilian wine. Now she was on her way to the home of one of her best friends. They often passed a pleasant afternoon together, whiling away the hours which would otherwise have been filled with aching loneliness.

She arrived at the stout wooden door set in an archway in the white wall, and knocked. The servant opened it and ushered her into the familiar shady courtyard, with its cushioned divans, marble statues, and plants in large terracotta pots.

Nerissa bustled towards her, and together they settled

comfortably under a potted fig tree, while the servant went to fetch clay goblets and wine. Chloe sighed with relief and flapped a handkerchief around her perspiring face.

"*Whew!*" she exclaimed. "I seem to feel the heat more these days!"

"Well, it will be winter soon," remarked Nerissa.

Chloe kicked off her sandals and prepared to indulge in some hearty gossip. "So what's new?" she asked. "I haven't seen you for a while."

Nerissa took a swig of wine and swallowed. Then she leaned forward confidentially. "Haven't you heard about those men from Judea?"

Chloe frowned. "Men from Judea? You mean those Jewish fellows who set up the synagogue here?"

"No, no!" Nerissa exclaimed impatiently. "No, *they've* been around for ages, with their long faces, and always spouting the Law and such. No, these guys are different. They seem to have been travelling all over Asia, teaching a new message. Very interesting!"

"Good-looking? Rich?" queried Chloe hopefully. "Young or old?"

"Oh, Chloe!" Nerissa laughed. "You don't change, do you?" She settled herself more comfortably, enjoying the advantage of being the first with the news. "Listen, this is what happened. I was at Quintus's and Damaris's house the other day. You may not know, but they've flirted a bit with going along to the synagogue, although they're not Jews. They say they're looking for something ..." Nerissa looked a bit vague for a moment, then continued: "Anyway, they said that a group of men turned up – they'd been in that boat that came into harbour last week."

"You mean that one full of Romans and prisoners?" said Chloe, somewhat dismissively.

"That's the one," nodded Nerissa. "They set out from Caesarea or somewhere a few weeks ago, and are hoping to get to Italy eventually, but the winds were against them and they only got as far as Salmone. They want to get to Phoenix for winter, so they came round this side. But I think they'll be stuck here in Fair Havens for a while yet."

"So what's so interesting about them?" murmured Chloe with her eyes closed.

"Well, Damaris said that a group of them were allowed off the boat to go to the synagogue. They brought greetings and then were invited to preach – and the service just came alive! Apparently, they said that some of the prophecies that the Jews are always going on about have come true. A man they claim to be the Messiah has come."

Chloe yawned and opened her eyes. "Should we care?" she asked. "I mean, Jewish prophecies ... What did the rabbis say?"

"Some people took it seriously, but the rabbis didn't like it," admitted Nerissa. "It caused a bit of a rumpus. But Quintus and Damaris seem really intrigued. So they've arranged for the men to come to their place tomorrow night and explain it some more!" Nerissa sat back and folded her hands over her stomach.

Chloe was thoughtfully silent for a few minutes, digesting it all, and then ventured, "So what is this teaching that's apparently so powerful?"

"Why don't you come with me tomorrow and find out?" suggested Nerissa. "Come here first and we'll go together."

The next evening, Chloe made sure to be at Nerissa's house in good time. Ever since she had been widowed five years before, Chloe's life had seemed dull and purposeless. She had got into the habit of drifting around from house to house with other women in a similar situation, all trying to fill the vacuum in their lives, eating too much, drinking too much, and talking volubly, unguardedly, often lewdly. Chloe sometimes felt ashamed in her sober moments, but didn't know how to change. Without a goal to pursue, there was no motivation to be different.

When the two women arrived at Quintus's large, spacious villa, it was getting dark. They were greeted and ushered through the atrium into the courtyard, where quite a crowd had already gathered. Glancing around, Chloe noticed a number of people she knew and was soon comfortably seated in a corner with some friends, while servants arranged seats in a semicircle.

There was a commotion at the door, and Quintus and Damaris hurried forward to welcome in a group of half a dozen men. They were conducted to seats in front of the semicircle. Quintus clapped his hands for attention and welcomed everyone, and then introduced the strangers.

A tall, patrician-looking man who identified himself as Luke, a Greek physician and historian, stood up and explained how they came to be there. It was a strange story. One of their number, Paul, was actually a prisoner under escort to Rome. They had embarked with him at Caesarea where he had been arrested for apparently inciting riots. (Chloe was slightly disappointed when he gestured towards a short man with dark eyes and thinning hair – he didn't look particularly villainous to her.) Luke said that the ship's captain had become quite friendly with Paul and treated him leniently, allowing him freedom of movement on the island of Crete, as long as he reported to him daily.

The tall man then introduced the rest of his companions. Chloe could only remember the names Trophimus from Ephesus, Silas from Antioch, and Titus, another Greek. She wondered why Paul's friends had chosen to come with him to Rome, sharing the deprivations of his captivity and the discomfort and perils of sea travel.

As if he read her thoughts, Luke explained that he and his companions had met Paul at various junctures of their lives and had been so impacted by the power of his teaching that it had changed their lifestyles for ever. He called this teaching "the gospel".

"Gospel". "Good news". This was not a new word. It was used to describe all sorts of things: victory over enemies, the end of war or famine, the arrival of a hero. What "good news" were these guys bringing? Chloe reached for her wine cup as the short man, Paul, began to speak.

She didn't touch her cup again, so transfixed was she by his mesmerizing message. Paul told the attentive company how he had been a model Jew, a Pharisee. So "righteous" was he that he had even hunted down those whom he considered to be wickedly deviant from the Jewish faith, and had them tortured and imprisoned. He called these heretics "Christians". They followed a man called Jesus, believing him to be the Messiah prophesied in their ancient Scriptures. (Here, Nerissa caught Chloe's eye, and winked.) He was apparently a good man, and performed miracles, but the orthodox Jews hated him because he upset all their ideas and traditions. Eventually he was crucified, and that should have been that ... except that, after a few weeks, his followers claimed he had not only risen from death, but had also filled them with his power.

Paul paused dramatically. Some members of his audience were a bit bewildered, but most were riveted. He described how he himself had been on his way to Damascus to round up these stupid Christians, when a dazzling light suddenly shone from heaven: Jesus himself had appeared to Paul and spoken to him!

There was a sharp intake of breath, and a ripple of amazement spread around the torchlit courtyard. Paul's voice grew soft as he remembered the words with which Jesus had called him and commissioned him to be a bearer of his message to the Gentiles: "I am sending you ... to open their eyes so that they may turn away from darkness to light and from the dominion of Satan to God, that they may receive forgiveness of sins and an inheritance among those who have been sanctified by faith in Me" (Acts 26:18).

With many other words, Paul went on to explain how this was relevant and significant for his hearers today on this island of Crete. They listened quietly and respectfully. Eventually, Quintus thanked Paul and told his guests they could depart, but some stayed to hear more. Paul, Luke and their companions promised to return to speak again if their ship was further delayed.

Chloe stood up and stretched her stiff limbs. Nerissa

took her arm and they went out into the moonlit street. Neither said much as they walked the short way back to Nerissa's house; both were affected by what they had heard and were not sure how to deal with it.

Nerissa offered to walk to Chloe's house with her, but Chloe declined. "I'll be all right," she said. The moon was shining bright as day; she could see her way quite clearly.

Uncharacteristically, Chloe wanted to be alone, to think, to puzzle over some of those things she had heard that evening.

In the morning, after a sleepless night, Chloe made up her mind. "I will find this man Paul, and ask him some questions." She made her way to Quintus's house, where Damaris received her kindly.

"You want to talk to Paul? You're not the only one!" Damaris remarked. "A lot of the guests who were here last night want to hear more. But I'm afraid we've just heard that the captain is impatient to leave. He thinks a fair wind is getting up, and they'll be able to make it to Phoenix in time for the winter. It's a much better harbour to stay in until spring."

Chloe was disappointed. How could Paul bring such teaching, only to leave them all dangling on a thread?

Damaris sighed. "I agree. I'm also longing to understand what this is all about. Perhaps Quintus could get a message to him? Or ..." Her voice trailed away. She looked at the hot, dumpy little woman in front of her, and felt compassion. Chloe had a reputation for skittering about, a frivolous, raucous party animal, with time on her hands. Damaris, a respectable mother, and wife of a distinguished citizen, had had little contact with her until recently. But now that they had both heard this message called the "gospel", they were somehow drawn together.

Some weeks passed. Then one day, Chloe was spending a languid afternoon drinking with Nerissa and some of her cronies, when one of them said, "My son met a traveller called Titus yesterday. He'd just come from Phoenix. Wanted to find Quintus."

Titus! The name impressed itself on Chloe. Wasn't one of Paul's friends called Titus? She turned to Nerissa. "Do you remember that evening at Quintus's house? I wonder if this is the Titus who was with those guys."

"*Hmm* ... bit of a long shot, if you ask me!" snorted Nerissa. "Still, you could go and find out, I suppose." She gave Chloe a sidelong glance. Her old friend had seemed a bit subdued ever since that night.

The next day, Chloe called at Quintus's villa. When Damaris appeared, Chloe felt foolish but blurted out that a rumour was going around: a traveller called Titus had returned from Phoenix – could he by any chance be one of the men who came with Paul? "I would so like to hear more of the message they brought," she explained.

To her relief, Damaris confirmed that he was indeed the same man. He had been sent back by Paul, who had realized that a lot of interest had been stirred up after the meeting in Quintus's home.

Titus proved to be a friendly, warm, likable man, full of enthusiasm and with a gift for explaining the gospel. He had travelled widely in the Mediterranean countries with Paul, and was therefore familiar with Paul's ways and teaching. Meetings at the villa became a regular occurrence, and it was not long before Chloe, along with Quintus and

Damaris, and Nerissa and several others, prayed with Titus, confessing their sins, and received the saving grace of God through Jesus.

Gradually, others joined them. Titus baptized them in water and began to teach them foundational truths and the implications of living as Christians. It was an exciting but also an uphill task. He often groaned to himself as he tried to make his bunch of converts understand the simplest things. These Cretans! They seemed to be content to lie around in the sun, drinking wine!

It wasn't long before the "Judaizers" showed up, just to complicate matters; these men were insisting on full obedience to the Jewish Law. Titus was trying to explain grace, yet at the same time instil some sense of discipline into his converts! He thought about Chloe and Nerissa, two widowed women whose lazy lifestyle seemed so at variance with the zeal and appetite for God which he had seen exhibited in other Greek women who had embraced the gospel – women like Priscilla and Phoebe, whom he had met in Ephesus.

He wrote despairingly to Paul: "What am I going to do with this lot? The old women sit around gossiping and drinking, while the Judaizers are seducing whole households with their insistence on Law and circumcision as a means of salvation."

Paul wrote back with helpful advice: "The reason I left you in Crete was so that you could carry on what we began there." He agreed with Titus' unflattering impressions of the local people, remembering that even a prominent Cretan had written that his fellow-islanders were "liars, brutes and lazy gluttons". *The man was right,* Paul thought! He forthrightly exhorted Titus not to be easy-going on them.

As for the Judaizers, Paul had no time for them at all. "They claim to know God, but by their actions they deny him. They are detestable, disobedient, unfit for doing any good."

Titus chuckled as he read Paul's thoroughgoing assessment; he could just imagine the energetic apostle waving his arms about as he dictated the letter. Then he sighed. At least he had permission to be decisive, but it was not going to be easy!

He read on. Paul left no stone unturned as he advised his young disciple on how to deal with the old men, the young men, the older women and young women, and the slaves; what to teach, what to emphasize, what to avoid.

Titus read and reread the epistle. As he became increasingly familiar with it, several things began to stand out. He soon knew by heart the things that Paul considered necessary for the establishment of a strong church: good leadership, suppression of false doctrine, teaching on the grace of God, pastoral advice for every age group. He worked hard to put these things in place. But he also realized that he would have to harness the experience and encourage the gifting of each age group.

His mind went to Chloe, thinking of Paul's admonitions: "Older women ... are to be reverent in their behaviour, not malicious gossips nor enslaved to much wine, teaching what is good." Chloe was irreverent, gossipy, addicted to wine. Could he help her come to a place of "teaching what is good"? Indeed, could he see her able to "encourage the young women to love their husbands, to love their children, to be sensible, pure, workers at home, kind, being subject to their husbands"? As he prayed over his flock, he tried to see them in a different light, to see, with faith, what they could become.

He and his wife, Hermia, prayed continually for each of their new converts and one day she came up with an idea. "Paul says that you should teach the older women how to behave so that they in turn can train the younger women. Perhaps you and I could get some of these older women together and try to help them."

"I think it would be more appropriate if *you* did that!" responded Titus.

His wife quailed at the thought. "Not me! I'm too young!" she protested.

"Maybe in years, but not in knowing Jesus," he pointed out.

Hermia had come with Titus from mainland Greece. She knew many mature Christian women such as Priscilla, and Timothy's mother Lois, and his grandmother Eunice. Their devoted training of Timothy had helped to shape him to become a fine Christian leader. Hermia found that, as she remembered these women, they furnished her with excellent examples of godly womanhood; they exemplified the very things Paul had directed Titus to teach. She wondered if Paul had had them in mind when he directed Titus to have the older women teach the younger ones how to love their husbands, how to love their children, be good homemakers, kind and pure. Paul must have stayed in many homes on his travels and enjoyed or endured varying degrees of hospitality!

He must have observed the well-run home where the wife, in harmonious accord with her husband, trained her children with loving discipline, and made her guests welcome in an ambience that was both relaxed and orderly. Such women were an asset in any church. They had serving hearts and generous natures, even if they were not rich by worldly standards. In his letter to the church in Rome, Paul had written affectionate greetings to many of the saints, including a man called Rufus "and his mother, who has been a mother to me, too". He had also commended several other women by name such as Tryphaena and Tryphosa (were they twins?), Mary, and Persis, all of whom he said "worked hard" (Romans 16:6, 12–13). Evidently, the apostle approved of women who were industrious!

Hermia wondered if Paul had also stayed in households where the wife and husband were at odds, the children insecure and unhappy, and the guests awkwardly tiptoeing around in a tense atmosphere. Such households did not adorn the gospel!

That was the point, mused Hermia with sudden illumination, as she reflected on a phrase in the apostle's letter to her husband. "Older women ... are to ... encourage the young women ... so that the word of God *will not be dishonoured.*" This brought a whole new motivation! So Paul was not urging that these things be taught simply so that women should come into line, producing well-behaved children, nice, quiet homes and peaceful marriages, just to give everyone an easier life! It was much, much bigger than that.

Hermia took a deep breath as the enormity of the responsibility began to dawn on her. This teaching was not only about ensuring the health and well-being of the men, women and families in the church for their own sake: it was also about communicating their lifestyles to others around them.

That evening, after dinner, she began to share with Titus how her thinking was developing. He picked up the scroll from Paul, and searched for the phrase. "The same idea is repeated here ... and here!" he exclaimed. "Listen: 'Teach the young men ...' *Uh*, no, here it is: 'Teach the slaves ... so that in every way they will make the teaching about God our Saviour attractive.' So as you say, Paul isn't only concerned that we have nice homes. The way we run our marriages, homes and families also communicates things about God."

"What do you think it means, when he writes about dishonouring the word of God? How could we do that?" asked Hermia thoughtfully.

The teacher rose up in Titus. "Let's take that phrase, 'the word of God'," he said. "Where else have we heard that?"

Hermia shook her head. She was a Greek woman, not versed in the Hebrew Scriptures. But Titus had sat at Paul's feet, and heard him expound from the book of Genesis, and right through the Old Testament.

"In the beginning, God spoke and things sprang into being that were not there before," her husband explained. "God's word is active and powerful. When he says something, things happen! Things are made, or they change, or are strengthened." He jumped to his feet and began to pace about. "We learn lots of other things about the word from the Jewish Scriptures. Isaiah prophesied about God's word, that it is like the rain and the snow which come down and water the earth, so that it brings forth its fruit. He said, 'So will *My word* be which goes forth from My mouth. It will not return to Me empty, without accomplishing what I desire.'"

Hermia nodded. She was with him so far.

He came back and sat down beside her on the couch, and took her hands. "Now, Hermia, who else talks about the Word, the *Logos*?"

That was a Greek word she knew, of course. "I think I've heard you say that the apostle John teaches that Jesus is the Word ... Oh!" Realization began to grip her. "Jesus is what God wants to say to us!"

"Exactly," said Titus softly. "Just as the rain comes down from heaven, so Jesus came from the Father. And he ascended back to the Father, not empty-handed, but having accomplished the Father's will completely."

"'It is finished'," murmured Hermia. "Yes, I see. He did everything the Father intended him to do. No wonder he said, 'The Father abiding in Me does His works.' She was quiet. Then, "So the Word of God is not just words; it is a person: Jesus."

"Yes. Jesus embodies what God wants to express to the world," said Titus, "so when we act contrary to what God says, we dishonour Jesus."

Hermia blinked. Something that she already vaguely understood was coming into sharper focus. "So the sort of woman I am can make it easier or harder for people to see something of Jesus, and be drawn to God."

Armed with this thought, Hermia felt even more motivated to teach the women. Her job was not just to try and make them more "moral", or to have happier lives;

it was to bring to them a sense of purpose, which was to honour Jesus.

A few days later, she and Damaris, Chloe and Nerissa were sitting in her garden, and while her two infants played around their feet, she began to share her discovery with her friends.

"How do you think, in view of this, that as women we could bring dishonour to the Lord Jesus?"

"Dishonour!" exclaimed Nerissa. "That's quite a strong word, isn't it?" The others nodded.

"What other words could we use, then?" asked Damaris. "What does 'dishonour' mean?"

Hesitantly, Chloe offered, "Lack of respect? Not taking someone seriously?"

The others chimed in: "What about malign? Speak ill of someone?"

"Trivialize?"

"Count as unimportant?"

They sat back and looked at each other soberly. So the way they lived could make people think that the Jesus they professed was unimportant, or worse!

Hermia pushed it further. "So what things dishonour Jesus?" she persisted. "Paul says he wants women to love their husbands, love their children, be self-controlled, kind, pure ... all those things."

"I guess we need to find out how he wants us to conduct our marriages and order our homes, then." This from Damaris.

"But what about us?" questioned Chloe. "Nerissa and I don't have husbands any more. Nerissa has grown-up children, of course, but I don't even have those!"

Hermia went over to her and took her hand.

"Dear Chloe!" she said warmly. "There are so many ways you can bring honour to Jesus. You could welcome lonely people to your home; you could help young mums who are tired and discouraged. And you don't have to have children of your own to be a mother! I'm sure if you asked the Lord about it, he would show you lots of ways you could honour him." Hermia remembered Phoebe, a single lady from Cenchrea whom she had once met, who had a loving, serving heart. She wished Chloe could meet her.

"I know!" exclaimed Damaris. "Let's take each of these things that Paul says we should do, and talk and think about them carefully. Maybe we could invite some of the other women to join us."

The others were enthusiastic and so began a regular event. The women took hold of Paul's epistle and set about exploring the way God wanted them to live.

They discovered that he was not advocating rules; he wanted them to live in the grace of God. It was the grace of God that instructed them to say "No" to temptation, and "Yes" to the nudges of the Spirit. They were not to be motivated by fear of failure, or fear of punishment, or fear of breaking a self-imposed standard. They were to be spurred on by the love and grace of God, which taught them to see themselves as forgiven, clean, free and valued by him. It also taught them to see others as precious to God, having dignity and worth, and to treat them accordingly, whether they were husbands, children, friends or leaders.

As time went on, Chloe's lifestyle began to change. She was no longer drifting aimlessly through life: she had purpose. When she woke up in the morning, she was happily aware that the presence of Jesus brought promise to her day. She began to see her home in a different light: it was no longer just her home, it was his! She began to take a pride in it, to tidy it, clean it, fill vases with fresh flowers, and throw out accumulated junk which had been lying around gathering dust ever since her husband died. She got rid of dead plants in the courtyard, bought some new ones and planted them in beautiful pots, tastefully grouped near the door. She went to the market and purchased some colourful rugs, and rearranged the furniture. She felt Jesus' pleasure as her unique creativity asserted itself: something else which he had put in her!

All this unaccustomed activity made her tired. She found she was sleeping much better, eating less and beginning to lose some of the bulging fat around her midriff. As she worked happily to make her home more attractive, and also made friends in the new church, attending Sunday services and the women's discussion group, her life became fuller and more fulfilling. Drinking wine became simply an enjoyable occasional accompaniment to a meal, not an end in itself.

The day came when she shyly volunteered to host the women's discussion group in her home. Formerly, she would have been ashamed to have anyone visit her and see the chaos she lived in, but now she was glad to open her door to her friends.

One day, as the church was gathering for worship, Hermia came over to her, leading a young woman by the hand.

"Chloe, I want you to meet Sophia," she said. "She has just become a Christian, but has lots of questions. I thought you would be just the person to help her!"

Chloe was dumbfounded, but before she could protest, Hermia smiled and said, "Just share your story with her. Tell her how Jesus helped you see your life differently."

"I would love to!" responded Chloe. She turned to Sophia and smiled. "How about tomorrow afternoon?" she asked.

Questions for group discussion

- **What goals should we be pursuing in discipling one another?**
- **What should discipling *not* be?**
- **What should a disciple be expecting from an "older" woman?**
- **What boundaries, if any, should be established?**

CHAPTER 3

A Devious Woman

> *A man named Ananias, with his wife Sapphira, sold a piece of property, and kept back some of the price for himself, with his wife's full knowledge, and bringing a portion of it, he laid it at the apostles' feet.*
>
> Acts 5:1–12

It's home-group night, thought Sapphira. *I'd better make sure that supper is ready when Ananias comes in or we'll be late.* As she busied herself with chopping and stirring, she thought about the people in the group, especially about the elder who was coming that night: Barnabas.

Everyone liked Barnabas. *I wonder why?* thought Sapphira. Surely it was because he loved people. He consoled them when they were down, and laughed with them when they were happy. He patiently instructed them and sometimes gently corrected them when they needed to adjust their attitude. Sapphira found him slightly intimidating; he could be very straight and she wasn't used to that. She and Ananias had become adept at dodging issues and wriggling out of tight spots. Like nearly all weak and fallible human beings, they wanted to be liked and admired. This was not wrong in itself, but they had not learned that friendships and reputations are built, not on showy impressions and shallow gestures, but on strength of character.

What Sapphira did not recognize was the major difference between Barnabas's attitude and theirs. While he was utterly trustworthy and his word totally reliable, they got away with whatever they could. Their word was frequently questionable. Indeed, their concept of truth often turned out to be somewhat flexible.

Barnabas was a good "shepherd". He looked after the "lame sheep" of his flock and prayed for their health. He tried to affirm Ananias and Sapphira and win their confidence, and bring them to a place of safety where they could admit their needs without fear. But they lacked the courage to confront the truth about themselves. They were certainly Christians; they were saved. But instead of trusting the new river of life from within, they continued to drink from the old, polluted stream. It was this stream which warned them, *Don't abandon yourselves completely to this new way. Who knows where it will lead? Keep your options open! Give the appearance of being wholehearted, but keep something in reserve. Look out for number one!*

Barnabas tried hard to lead the couple into a deeper trust in the Lord and his word, but they did not respond well. The pure river of life was muddied by the other stream and the fruit it produced was poisonous: lies, evasion, compromise and argumentativeness.

Meanwhile, the church was having a glorious time. People from all walks of life were being added daily, flawed and broken individuals were receiving mercy and forgiveness, lives were changing. Healings and miracles were taking place and joy abounded. God's rule was being displayed in righteousness and peace. The new believers were deepening in spiritual maturity as they received the apostles' teaching, and as they prayed and broke bread together, working out their commitment to one another in daily life. They were not only zealous to share the good news of the gospel; they were also keen to share their material possessions.

Though most people thrived in this atmosphere, one or two like Ananias and Sapphira felt threatened by such close and wholehearted fellowship. They were afraid that their secret weaknesses would be exposed and that they would no longer be acceptable. Their fear of rejection kept them on the fringe; they knew too much to leave altogether, but were wary of being totally involved. Many of the new Christians were fairly poor, so they did not lose much by pooling their possessions; in fact, they gained quite considerably. Those who were wealthier expressed their commitment to the Lord by providing for many orphans, widows and other unfortunate people. They gave joyfully because they did not regard their possessions as things they should keep to themselves; rather, they had all things in common. It was rumoured that Barnabas had sold a valuable plot of land and had laid the entire proceeds at the feet of the apostles, trusting them to make best use of the money.

Ananias and Sapphira were round-eyed with wonder as they digested this latest morsel of news. Barnabas went up another notch in their estimation. It was of particular interest to them because they too were negotiating the sale of some land. However, they now felt somewhat under pressure. If it became known that they had sold the land

and kept all the money, would they not be compared with Barnabas and judged for not being as generous as he?

Their admiration for Barnabas became mingled with irritation: the example he was setting was too high for them. Yet what a glorious gesture! It was an act for which he deserved applause and honour, and they envied him the esteem and recognition that it brought him. How desirable to gain that sort of respect, to be put in the same bracket as dignified, popular Barnabas!

As negotiations for their land continued, Ananias and Sapphira discussed what they should do with the money that the sale would bring them.

"We could give it all away, you know," said Sapphira bluntly, one night. "After all, we're managing all right on our present income. If we keep it, we're liable to be taxed on it anyway."

Ananias frowned uneasily. "I'm not sure," he admitted. "We're talking about an awful lot of money. And we did inherit the plot from my mother. Is that what she would have wanted?"

Sapphira sidestepped the red herring. "Well, then, what shall we do with it?" she asked, then added some practical suggestions. "I'd love some new clothes; we could have a good holiday and invest the rest for our grandchildren."

This horrified Ananias. "What would Peter and Barnabas and all the rest think of that?" he exclaimed, ever watchful of his image. "It would seem too self-indulgent for words – not very spiritual! You know, the Christian life is all about taking up your cross and denying yourself, not about going on holiday. I'd never be seriously considered for leadership!"

"Well, then," continued his wife, "if you don't want to give it all away, or spend it, why not give some *and* keep some?"

But to small-minded Ananias, the initial answer to that was, "It just wouldn't look so good." He badly wanted to be esteemed and accepted like Barnabas, but he was unwilling to pay the price; to become a man of integrity required being wholehearted. He wanted to have his cake and eat it, to be part of the body but retain independence, to follow the Lord but not take up the cross, to have eternal life but not die to self.

Once again, compromise came to his aid. Yes, he would do as his wife suggested: give some and keep some. There was no harm in that. "But there's no need to tell anyone that we kept some," he told her. "Let them think we gave the whole lot!"

Sapphira looked at him through narrowed eyes. She knew exactly what was going on in the mind of this man of hers. He was not an "all or nothing" man. He lived on his wits, shrewd but weak, making sure there was always something to fall back on.

***

At this point, Ananias and Sapphira could have broken free. They could have decided to be open and honest. Was heaven holding its breath, waiting for a change of heart? It wasn't so much what they did with the money that mattered. In fact, they had three legitimate alternatives. They could abandon their fear, trust in a God who has promised blessings without number, and gladly give it all away. Or they could thank God for it, and happily, without fear of judgement, keep it all. Or they could openly share some of the proceeds with their brothers and sisters.

The One who owns the cattle on a thousand hills and can turn stones into bread was not particularly concerned about the money! Of far greater concern to God were the motives of their hearts. Would they allow themselves to be moulded in his hands into the image of his Son? Would they walk out of the "twilight zone" of cunning and deceit into the light? Would they learn to seek God honestly for his will regarding the money and then do what he said?

The Lord could not endorse a gift tainted by his old Enemy, the Serpent, the source of deception. It was he who was the father of lies, who bent truth, and sought to warp integrity and twist righteousness. The Lord Jesus had come to make the crooked straight, after all.

Oh, Ananias and Sapphira, be alert to the wiles of the Enemy! Don't defile the early church!

***

Sapphira drew a deep breath and looked Ananias in the eye. "I won't tell if you won't," she promised.

A few weeks later, Sapphira walked confidently into the room where the church was gathered for prayer. The men had been meeting in the morning and the women planned to join them after lunch. After a few paces, she stopped uncertainly. Something was horribly wrong!

Peter came up to her and placed his hand on her shoulder. Every eye was on her. She looked around nervously, her eyes seeking Ananias, but she couldn't see him in the crowd.

"Sapphira," said Peter, "I want to ask you a question."

He was so serious! What was going on?

"Tell me ..." he said, "... when you and Ananias sold your land and brought the money to the leaders, was that *all* the money you got for it?"

They suspect! she thought. *But how did they guess?* Her eyes darted round the room. She swallowed and tried to control her shaking hands as her mind ran frantically through the possible answers. *If I say, "No, we kept some," then our gift won't seem so noble and we'll look mean and stingy; but if I say, "Yes," we'll look stupid if we're caught out as liars! Anyway, Ananias and I have agreed on our story. I can't back out now, it would be too embarrassing. And Ananias would be furious! Where on earth is he?* She was irritated with Ananias for getting her into this impossible situation, leaving her to deal with it on her own.

I suppose he made himself scarce when he realized that someone suspected we'd held some money back! she thought. *Well, I'd better stick to our story and try to bluff it out.*

Sapphira tossed back her head and forced a smile. "Yes!" she said clearly. "That was the full price!"

Instantly, she knew she had said the wrong thing. There was an intense, suffocating silence. Peter sighed deeply.

"Why did you invent this story?" he demanded. "Do you really think you can deliberately attempt to deceive the church and get away with it? You're not just lying to us, you are lying to the Holy Spirit! He will not condone deception!"

Sapphira looked at him dumbly, shocked into a new

understanding of the seriousness of their action. In all their discussions, she and Ananias had never considered that "bending the truth" meant sinning against the Holy Spirit. Never had they thought that lying to the body of Christ would dishonour the One who proclaimed, "I am the truth." They had simply been preoccupied with their own image and security. It had never occurred to them that the church, which was destined to be holy, righteous and undefiled, would be infected by the poison of deceit.

She heard footsteps outside. Peter also heard them.

"The men are returning from the cemetery," he told her. "They have been burying your husband, and they will soon carry you out and bury you too."

Instantly, Sapphira dropped to the floor, dead. The group of men came in and wound a sheet around her; they carried her out and buried her next to her husband in the grave they had dug three hours before.

***

The apostle Peter here declared God's judgement on lies, deception and compromise. The sceptre of righteousness is the sceptre of his kingdom. The church must be the agent by which the Lord establishes his government, the city set on a hill which declares his standards of living, a light in a dark world, a lily among thorns. A church that compromises that purity and tolerates what is basically anti-God is not so much a lily as a bramble masquerading as a lily. It is also confusing to those who, thinking they have found a lily, reach out to it, only to become torn and disillusioned. It is vital for every member of God's church to be clean, wholehearted and honest.

This story also shows that each person stands or falls by her own actions. Sapphira was a collaborator with her husband in his sin. She could have tried to dissuade him, or refused to be a party to the deception. Peter sternly rebuked her for conspiring with him; it would have been useless, then, if she had tried to protest that she was submitting to her husband, that it was all his fault. Submission is not a "get-out clause"! God never asks wives to submit to their husbands if to do so would mean participating in sin.

Sadly, this couple's motives were so mixed and muddled that what could have been a commendable act became nauseating to God and endangered the health of the vigorous young church, beautiful in its new life.

Questions for group discussion

- **What was Sapphira's sin?**
- **How should we give to God's work?**
- **Is it ever right to keep something back from God's work?**
- **Why do you think the judgement in this story was so severe?**

CHAPTER 4

A Dead Woman Raised to Life

Acts 9:36–43

Tabitha bit off the thread and folded the garment with relief. Another one finished! She felt so tired these days, and it was becoming increasingly difficult to see clearly. Slowly, she got up from her chair and stretched her cramped limbs. It was early evening and the light was fading. She was glad to have finished the tunic before darkness fell completely.

She lived in Joppa, a small fishing town on the Mediterranean coast. A few years ago, a man called Peter had come with exciting news. Some of the fishermen in the village knew him because he also was a fisherman, from Galilee, an inland lake with a thriving fishing industry in the towns around its shores. Peter had not done much fishing for several years because he had become the disciple of a rabbi called Jesus and had been following him around. Some of his friends had heard about this teacher; his fame had spread beyond Galilee and Judea – it was said he could heal the sick. In fact, some had seen him when they had had occasion to go up to Jerusalem.

One evening, Peter had arrived in Joppa and found some of his old friends. He told them that the rabbi had been wrongly accused and condemned to death by crucifixion. His friends murmured in horror. They had heard some of the rumours that had been flying around. Such a cruel death! Those Romans! Peter went on to describe how the man had been buried in a tomb. Then he and others had gone to the tomb after the Sabbath, and found it open and empty! Peter had gone in himself and had taken a look. Then suddenly, the dead man appeared! He was no ghost, Peter explained, but very much alive, and was seen by many other people.

Peter explained the implications of this. He believed that the man was the Messiah, promised in the Scriptures by the prophets. With many convincing arguments he won over many of his friends, and soon a little band of believers grew. Tabitha, a widow, heard the good news, believed, and joined them. This little group was now her family! She was overjoyed with the gospel message, but also thrilled that she was surrounded by loving people. Her solitary days were over.

The people of Joppa lived meagre lives, relying on fishing for an income. It was a haphazard existence, and families lived close to the breadline. Tabitha was skilled with her needle and loved to help supplement their overstretched resources by mending and making garments. In return, she was invited to share meals, and was cared for by the embryonic church.

News began filtering to them of tumultuous happenings in Jerusalem. Many were becoming believers in Jesus, even priests, even Pharisees! But there was also strong opposition, and disciples were being imprisoned and tortured. One prominent leader, Stephen, had even been stoned to death. Christians began to scatter, fleeing from persecution, and as they did they took with them the good news of Jesus.

Peter travelled among the multiplying groups of believers in Judea, Galilee and Samaria, strengthening and encouraging the people. On one occasion, he went to Lydda, not far from Joppa, where he stayed for a few weeks (Acts 9:31–32). Extraordinary news was brought back to Joppa. There was a man called Aeneas who had been paralysed and bedridden for eight years. The Joppa Christians were dumbfounded to hear that Peter had commanded him to get up and walk in the name of Jesus ... and he did! Tabitha and her friends talked about this endlessly. They were hearing that other extraordinary miracles were happening through apostles in other places too.

Tabitha hummed contentedly as she gathered her sewing things together and put them away in a basket. Life was good! As she reached up to put the basket on the shelf, she swayed, suddenly dizzy and nauseous. She must sit down. She staggered to her bed, but when she lay down, she found she could not breathe properly and there was a pain in her chest, so after a few minutes she struggled to her feet. Frightened, she knew she must get help, so, gasping for breath, she tried to get to her door to call her neighbour. But the pain in her chest intensified. Everything went black as she crumpled to the floor.

That was where they found her the next morning. She had been dead for some hours by then. The news spread rapidly round the village, and weeping friends gathered in the bare little house. Tenderly, they washed her body and laid it out on the bed upstairs. More tears broke out as they discovered the little pile of newly finished shirts and tunics, neatly folded.

The young mother from next door sobbed, "What shall we do without her? She was so kind, so loving!" The sobs rose to a crescendo.

Suddenly, one of them shouted, "Isn't Peter in Lydda? Why don't we send for him? Perhaps he can do something."

The weeping abated as the friends all looked at one another. One shrugged and said, "Well, it can't do any harm."

But others began to talk excitedly. "Remember Aeneas? He was healed, wasn't he?"

"Yes, but this is different. Tabitha's dead!"

"Let's call Peter anyway!"

While they were discussing the idea, one woman ran and fetched a couple of the young men. They were very willing to go; it was not a good day for fishing and Lydda was not far. So they set off to find Peter.

They were soon back, Peter with them. He could hear the sounds of mourning long before he arrived at the house. At the doorway, hands grabbed him and dragged him up the stairs to the crowded chamber. Around the bed, the women were crying, and many of them were holding clothes that Tabitha had made, remembering her generosity and skill. It was chaos!

Peter surveyed the room. All he could see was hopelessness, despair and grief. He needed quiet and space, he needed to hear his Master's voice. He remembered entering a similar scene with Jesus, when Jairus's daughter had died. Gently but firmly, he told them all to leave the room. Reluctantly, they trickled out.

He turned now to the inert form on the bed. Yes, he remembered her: a cheerful, gentle little woman, kind-hearted, always sewing and doing things for other people. She looked smaller now, shrunken, so still – definitely dead. He knelt down at the bedside. What did Jesus want to do? Would he give Peter permission to call her back?

In his memory, Peter was back in Jairus's house, looking at the dead form of the little girl. "The Father abiding in Me does His works," Jesus had said. "He who believes in Me, the works that I do, he will do also; and greater works ..." What was the Father saying now? *You can ask anything in his name!* (John 14:10, 12, 13).

Peter straightened up and touched the dead woman's hand. "Tabitha," he said, "get up!"

Her eyelids fluttered, and she opened her eyes. When she saw Peter, she smiled. "Peter!" she exclaimed. "What are *you* doing here?" She sat up, and Peter helped her to her feet.

He opened the door and called, "You can all come in now!" But Tabitha was behind him at the top of the stairs, laughing gleefully at the astonished expressions on the faces of all her friends.

Not surprisingly, the news raced through the whole town and many believed in the Lord. Peter stayed on with a friend called Simon, who was a tanner by trade, to help disciple and establish the new believers.

***

Now, we may ask ourselves, why was Tabitha called back to life? Why not Stephen, a mighty man full of faith and the

Holy Spirit? He was stoned to death, but not raised to life. Tabitha was not a mighty woman as far as we know: just an ordinary person who liked sewing and helping people.

We cannot presume to know the answer to such a question. For one thing, God does not evaluate people as we do, on the basis of power and influence. And for another, he knows what a church most needs and where to deploy his personnel.

A few years ago, our dear friend Simon Pettit suddenly died of a heart attack in New Zealand. We had been at the celebration of his 50th birthday a few days before in Cape Town, South Africa. He was a giant of a man in every way. Tall and imposing, he had a personality to match, but was also a mighty man of faith, a preacher and church planter. We had thought him indispensable to the developing churches in Newfrontiers, not just in Africa, his main sphere of ministry, but all over the world. How could we live without him? How would the churches be able to function? The grief and sense of loss were overwhelming.

Some years later, we are marching on, but still feel the pain of losing him. However, despite the huge changes that took place as a result of his death, the work did not utterly cave in – although at times it was distinctly wobbly in places! It became the occasion for a lot of rethinking. Painful adjustments were the seedbed of new developments, as other people were forced to grow into their potential faster than they would otherwise have done. A mighty oak had fallen, but it was not a new oak tree that took its place. A bunch of saplings are growing in the gap that he left; the landscape has changed.

Was it like that when Stephen died? Certainly, his

martyrdom became the catalyst for taking the gospel beyond Jerusalem, as many believers fled the coming persecution, spreading their faith as they went. Stephen's fearless witness resulted indirectly in countless new converts.

What about Tabitha's resurrection? That also resulted in many new converts, as people heard of it and put their trust in a miracle-working God. The little church in Joppa presumably also rejoiced as she resumed her sewing ministry!

We can never determine who is more deserving of being healed or raised from the dead. The Christian life doesn't work like that. From our perspective, we can think of all sorts of good reasons why a person's life should be prolonged, and often our prayers for healing include these arguments. But God's arm is not twisted by our logic. God's desire is for the name of Jesus to be honoured and for his kingdom to be extended. Sometimes this happens when a person dies, sometimes when a person miraculously lives.

As I write, I receive news from one of our churches in the United Kingdom. A 40-year-old man was driving his van to work through a village, when he suddenly felt unwell. He managed to pull into the side of the road by a shop, and open the van door. He then fell out, and when the ambulance arrived he was pronounced dead. He was rushed to hospital where he was revived. In the meantime, he had died, and had met the Lord Jesus. His life is now radically changed; he has a new and fervent passion to share the gospel, and his personal love for Jesus has been fanned into a flame.

We must not become passive, adopting a "some you win, some you lose" attitude. "*Que sera sera*" is not in God's vocabulary. He wants us to stretch our faith, to become more expectant of his intervention, to ask for signs and wonders. If we want to be truly charismatic people – that is, people who believe in and desire the gifts distributed by the Holy Spirit – we must keep asking for more of the Spirit, and that includes more manifestations of his power. Speaking in tongues, interpretation and prophecy are some of the gifts he has given, and we have come to see these as part of the normal experience of a New Testament church. Healings are also on the increase. But how often do we pray for the gifts of faith, wisdom, miracles, works of power? "Pursue love, yet desire earnestly spiritual gifts" (1 Corinthians 14:1). I think we so often suspect our own motives that we are afraid to seek such things. Yet the word of God exhorts us to. "You do not have because you do not ask" (James 4:2).

The story of Tabitha shows us how much the Christians at Joppa loved this woman and how distraught they were at losing her. We tend to think that value in the local church is measured in terms of public ministry such as preaching, teaching or prophesying. Certainly, we do love and value these things. But we are told to "pursue love" as well as to "desire ... spiritual gifts". Tabitha pursued love by using her talents to bless others, and they loved her for it. Let us not cease to value every believer who uses her gifts to bless the family of God.

Peter was used here to bring about a mighty miracle; some may feel this was not so remarkable, as he was an apostle! Yet Paul's injunction to "desire earnestly spiritual gifts" was not restricted to apostles. It was written to a whole church, in fact to a church which had got a lot of things wrong, and was far from perfect!

In recent years, I have seen many people healed from a variety of sicknesses, frequently when my husband Terry has prayed for them and laid hands on them: back problems, incurable kidney disease, pains in necks and shoulders, chronic fatigue syndrome. One lady, who had had to use a wheelchair for 25 years because of a condition known as ataxia caused by brain disease, suddenly stood up and walked! The following day, she walked into church and stood to give her testimony. It was overwhelmingly moving. (At the time of writing, she continues to be well.)

We are learning that there is no particular formula that can be employed to guarantee healing. Paul wrote about "gifts of healing" (1 Corinthians 12:9) and it appears that some people grow in confidence when praying for particular conditions. For example, Terry has had faith for years to pray for back complaints. He is seeing increasing fruitfulness in praying for other skeletal complaints. Terry also seems to move in faith when he prays for individuals after he has preached. Sometimes he prays a "blanket" prayer (that is, over everyone) from the platform, but only a handful of people are healed. He finds more faith when sitting on the floor at the end of a meeting, praying for individuals.

Other friends of ours operate differently. Our Indian friend, Rambabu, speaks at vast meetings all over India, and increasingly all over the world. Primarily an evangelist, he preaches the gospel with great power. But often, before he preaches, he receives many words of knowledge, and people begin to experience amazing healings without him coming near them or praying specifically for them.

Basically, Rambabu is announcing the kingdom of God, and the healings are a sign of its coming.

Similarly, at Newday, a great youth camp run by Newfrontiers each summer, Adrian Holloway preaches the gospel and then prays from the platform for ill people to be healed. We have seen some astonishing things happen, as the power of God comes upon individuals, usually with no one touching them. Life-threatening allergies have disappeared; eye injuries and injured limbs have been healed.

The Scriptures also encourage elders to anoint people with oil and pray for them. The elders in my church, and in many other churches I know, regularly do this and have seen many healings, some of longstanding complaints.

One thing we must not do is to assume that the person who is used to bring the healing is imbued with supernatural power and knowledge, so that he or she is then viewed as a sort of guru on every spiritual subject. A gifted individual may not necessarily be a mature one. In the Old Testament, Samson had extraordinary power, but he was also an undisciplined, sensual man who did not use his gifting responsibly. At the same time, his gift was genuine. We have a hard time with this: we tend to think that a person who has been entrusted with enormous gifting must be exceptionally holy, that they have proved themselves worthy of it, earning it by prayer, fasting, giving, or by some huge sacrifice. When they subsequently do something which demonstrates that they are embarrassingly human, we grow disillusioned and conclude that the gift could not have been from God. But it undoubtedly was.

In the New Testament, Jesus healed the sick and then commanded his disciples to do likewise. They came back from their first efforts euphoric with success. But Jesus brought them down to earth by saying, effectively, "Just be thankful that you're saved! You are ordinary people who need forgiveness" (see Luke 10:20). They were still ignorant, fallible people capable of blunders and mistakes. They had not suddenly been transformed into founts of wisdom because Jesus had given them permission to heal. Sadly, but understandably, people who move in healing gifts are often put on a pedestal and expected to live on a different plane from everyone else. Consequently, there are ripples of disillusionment and confusion when they fall off. We must not allow these incidents to deter us from obeying Jesus by asking him to heal the sick.

As our world careers along its increasingly decadent path, it needs to hear the good news of Jesus the Saviour, Healer, and Baptizer in the Spirit. It also needs to see a community of people who are doing the same works as Jesus, "who went about doing good and healing all who were oppressed by the devil, for God was with Him" (Acts 10:38). We are the recipients of prophetic words which encourage us to believe that God is continuing to pour out his Spirit in the world, and we may expect to see his people moving more frequently in demonstrations of his power. Certainly, we are seeing more healings now than at any time I can remember. Let us keep asking, seeking and knocking in faith for more miraculous interventions wherever the gospel is preached!

And what became of Tabitha? Interestingly, incidents of people who have died and returned to life on earth are not as rare as we might think. Not surprisingly, this experience is so profoundly influential that the rest of their lives are lived in the light of it. I know one man who was fatally stung by a deadly poisonous jellyfish while diving off the coast of Mauritius. After being dead for about fifteen minutes, he was restored to life. This happened over 20 years ago, yet he can still barely speak of it without weeping, so deeply affected was he by the mercy of God. Once, when I asked him to describe what he had seen, I could hardly keep standing as he talked, such was the power of his words. He is a powerful evangelist and has brought thousands to Christ all over the world.

So it would not be surprising if Tabitha was used by God to bring others to know him, as she told what had happened to her. However, let us not forget that we, like Tabitha, also have a testimony of being brought from death to life. One day, we will go through the "curtain" as our human bodies die, but we shall forever be alive with the Lord. As Paul said, "Therefore, comfort one another with these words" (1 Thessalonians 4:18).

Questions for group discussion

- **When someone close to you falls sick, how do you pray for them? What do you expect to happen?**
- **Have you become cynical about praying for healing?**
- **Are you growing in faith for more supernatural healings?**
- **Have you ever heard of, or met, anyone who was raised from the dead? What struck you about them?**

CHAPTER 5

A Pioneering Woman

Acts 18–19

Leaving Rome

As the ship drew near to the quay, Priscilla busied herself with gathering the few bundles of possessions which she and Aquila had been able to pack hastily in the turmoil of leaving Rome. A few weeks before, they had joined the stream of other Jews forced out of their homes by a crazed emperor who was looking for a scapegoat on which to pin the blame for a fire which had engulfed huge portions of the city.

Cohorts of his guard had come storming into the Jewish quarter, dragging people out of their houses, looting and destroying them. Aquila had been alerted already, and he and Priscilla quickly closed their shop, and grabbed the canvas bags which held essentials. Hidden deep inside them, under Aquila's tools, were some small bags of coins. He cast a last look around the courtyard which had been his home and the centre of his successful tent-making business. Aquila had been born in Pontus in Asia Minor, but after many years in Rome regarded himself as a Roman. But there was no time for a sentimental farewell. Pushing Priscilla ahead of him, he locked the door of the house, then piled their bundles onto a small handcart.

They crossed the courtyard and went out into the street, pulled the gate shut and padlocked it.

The street was full of confused, angry and frightened people running hither and thither, shouting, piling up possessions. A child stood crying as a harassed young couple tried to balance their cooking pots on an already precarious load. Another man was trying to urge an old woman to climb onto a wagon, but she was refusing to leave. Further up the street, smoke billowed out of a shop. Broken tiles and bricks lay in the road, and gaping holes bore testimony to the violent entry of hordes of pillaging soldiers.

"Come quickly!" urged Aquila as Priscilla turned to help the distressed old lady. "There is no time!"

The couple set off as quickly as the fleeing crowd would allow. Behind them, they heard the sound of another wall crashing down amid cries and wails of despair.

Eventually, they arrived at Ostia on the coast. The harbour was thronged with panicking Jews all trying to escape by sea. Aquila and Priscilla managed to obtain passage on a ship bound for Corinth.

It was a miserable voyage. People were distressed at the enforced evacuation. In their hurry, they had had little opportunity to gather their possessions or make decisions about their property, and most were simply taking what they could carry in bundles on their backs. Many had been separated from family members; some had had to leave behind elderly relatives. Priscilla suddenly found herself grateful that she had no children,[1] as she watched distressed mothers trying to console and care for little ones who were frightened and exhausted. Now in her mid-30s,

---

1 We don't know this for sure but surmise it from the lack of any reference to family every time she and Aquila are mentioned.

and married for 18 years, she knew it was unlikely now that she would ever have a family; yet she was grateful for health and vigour, enabling her to be a true partner to her hardworking husband.

As the ship drew into port after days at sea, the refugee passengers gazed apprehensively at the scene. The approach to Corinth was through a long, narrowing inlet. Sailing towards the harbour, they began to discern houses clustered closely on both sides and a massive and precipitous cliff dominating the town. The ship tied up at the quay and the passengers disembarked, dragging their pathetic bundles. Many simply stood and looked around, uncertainty written on their faces.

Corinth

Priscilla felt her spirits lift. It was good to get off that wretched boat and stretch her legs. All around her, in the heat of the afternoon, was colour and noise. She picked up and identified words from different languages: Persian and Aramaic, as well as the indigenous Greek, and others totally unknown to her. She smiled at Aquila and took his hand. "This is an interesting place," she said.

"Let's look for an inn to stay in tonight," Aquila suggested, "and then tomorrow we can begin to find our way around the city."

The next day, they began to look for a suitable place to set up their tent-making business. It took a couple of weeks, during which time they carefully spent as little as they could of their savings. It would cost a fair amount not only to rent or buy premises, but also to buy the skins and other materials for making tents and leather goods. They had to make a fresh start, but at least they had experience and energy. Aquila had decided to diversify into making bags and other leather goods as well as tents. These required fewer resources to make, and were likely to sell more quickly.

Gradually, they found their way around town, and began to make friends and adjust to the different customs. Much to their joy they found a synagogue, where they were welcomed, and so they became part of the community. Other Jewish refugees had also arrived and the congregation swelled considerably. As time went by, the trauma of their hurried eviction from Rome receded and they settled down to life in Corinth. After the first few rocky months, their business was established, and Priscilla applied herself not only to helping Aquila but also to making their home comfortable and hospitable.

She was stirring an appetizing stew one evening, when Aquila came in with a stranger. The man looked tired and travel-stained, Priscilla thought. He was slightly shorter than average for a male, in fact about the same height as Priscilla herself. She judged him to be in his mid-50s, although later she found out that he was about ten years younger. His travels had included some gruelling experiences which had aged him.

"This is Saul, from Tarsus," Aquila announced. It seemed that Saul had been standing outside the shop fingering some soft leather, when Aquila came out and they started talking. Saul soon divulged that he also was a tent-maker by trade, so they had a lot in common. He was also a Jew.

"My friends call me Paul," he said and invited them to do the same. They smiled, recognizing his nickname as a play on the Latin *paulus*, meaning "small". His voice was cultured, with a Hebrew accent. He spoke fluent Greek and Latin, although his native tongue was Aramaic. Priscilla and Aquila were more at home in Latin but were improving steadily in Greek. He seemed to have been travelling widely around the Mediterranean, and had only just arrived in Corinth.

Naturally, Priscilla and Aquila urged Paul to share their meal and, by the end of it, they all felt very easy and relaxed with one another. Priscilla and Aquila were a bit puzzled by some of the things he said, but since they were persuaded that he was, or had been, a Pharisee, they thought he must be orthodox. They told him where the synagogue was so that he could go there on the Sabbath.

It suddenly occurred to Priscilla, remembering their own first night in this city, that Paul might not have lodgings. She tried to catch her husband's eye, but he was already ahead of her.

"Are you going to an inn?" Aquila asked. "Because if you have no other arrangements, you can stay with us."

Gratefully, Paul accepted, and so began a long and fruitful friendship.

The next morning, it seemed natural for Paul to apply his skills in the couple's shop. He worked for Aquila for several months, and continued to lodge with them. He needed to earn some money, and Aquila was appreciative of his expertise.

On the Sabbath, they all went along to the synagogue. As a visitor, and especially as a former rabbi, Paul was invited to read the Scriptures and comment on them. This he did, but took the opportunity to explain that all that was written in the Mosaic Law and the Prophets was pointing toward the coming of the Messiah. The grey heads of the elders in the circle of men nodded solemnly, their fingers stroking their long beards. This much was known.

Paul's next words electrified them: "The Messiah is none other than Jesus of Nazareth whom I serve. He was a rabbi in Galilee, who went about doing good and healing all who were oppressed of the devil. Wicked men, jealous and angry, opposed him, saying he was a blasphemer. They took him to the Romans who gave him an unfair trial and had him executed by crucifixion. He died. But, like a sacrificial lamb, he was without sin, yet carrying our sin! He was buried in a tomb, but after three days was seen by many people, alive from the dead. I also am a witness, for he appeared to me, and forgave me all my sin. He is the Son of God!"

There was a stunned silence, then pandemonium broke out.

"Blasphemy!"

"How can this man say such things?"

"Be quiet and let him finish!"

"I don't want to hear any more of this."

"Well, I do – I want to know how he can be so sure he's telling the truth."

"The *truth*?"

Priscilla, sitting above in the women's gallery, watched transfixed as the normally sedate men, gesticulating wildly, yelled at each other. Crispus, the ruler of the synagogue, arose and managed to make himself heard.

"Men! Brethren! Calm yourselves! Let us not be hasty! As our visitor has said, the Scriptures do indeed speak of the coming Messiah. How can we know whether this man Jesus is the Messiah or not? Let us take time to examine these things! If it turns out to be nonsense, then we will act accordingly, but if not, we must be prepared to have open hearts."

Crispus's words carried weight and the congregation dispersed.

Paul went home with Priscilla and Aquila, where they questioned him eagerly on the claims he had made, until late in the evening. Eventually, Aquila yawned. "We must go to bed; we have work to do tomorrow," he said. "But we'll talk more about this!"

In bed, Priscilla was far too excited to sleep. Aquila was soon snoring at her side, but she stared into the darkness, turning over in her mind the things Paul had spoken of. Perhaps this was their destiny, the reason they had come here: to meet Paul and hear about this man Jesus of Nazareth.

***

It is possible that Priscilla and Aquila were more disposed than other Jewish expatriates to open their minds and then their hearts to the gospel. Many Jews had established little enclaves far away from Jerusalem and were committed to maintaining the old Judaist ways (in rather the same way that British colonials, centuries later, would try to keep up English customs in far-flung outposts of the empire, such as taking tea at four o'clock, changing one's clothes for dinner, and carrying umbrellas). Priscilla and Aquila, however, had come from cosmopolitan Rome, a seething town of many nationalities and philosophies, where Jewish ideals had possibly become diluted by the influence of other cultures.

***

It was not long before Priscilla and Aquila were persuaded that the Jesus whom Paul preached really was the Son of God. Later in life, Priscilla vividly remembered the day when she and Aquila knelt together and wholeheartedly committed their lives to following Jesus Christ of Nazareth.

They were not the only ones. Others from the synagogue, including Crispus and his entire family, also became Christians and were baptized. Paul was preaching in the synagogue every Sabbath, explaining the gospel with compelling power.

One day, Paul came home happy and excited, accompanied by two men whom he introduced as Silas and Timothy. They had been travelling down the eastern coast of Greece from Philippi where Paul had left them. It was evident that they were very dear and special friends, and the reunion was exuberant. Naturally, they all enjoyed the hospitality of Priscilla's table that night. Soon after that, Paul became so occupied with preaching that he had to stop working in Aquila's business. Silas and Timothy had brought a gift of money with them from the church in Philippi which helped to cover Paul's needs, and theirs, so he no longer needed to work to support himself.

The three men hired some rooms nearby to live in, a somewhat chaotic headquarters. The hospitable Priscilla was sad that Paul would no longer be staying in her home, but it soon became obvious that the preachers had little time or skill to look after their own daily needs, so they were often found at Priscilla's table, enjoying her excellent cooking. This was what Priscilla really enjoyed: using her home to make others feel loved and welcome, a setting where ideas could be exchanged and the mind stimulated, while the body was being nurtured.

It had become increasingly obvious that a large split was occurring in the synagogue between those who embraced the gospel of Jesus and those who opposed it. The opposition became increasingly vehement and threatening, so Paul left and rented a large hall nearby and carried on preaching. Now he was evangelizing on a broader front, not just to Jews, but to Greeks and indeed to people of all nationalities in the city, and not just on the Sabbath, but on weekdays as well.

Those were exciting days! Priscilla found herself much occupied, not only with the tent-making business, but with providing hospitality to many new people who were flocking to hear Paul preach. Usually, after lunch, she and Aquila shut the shop and went over the road to the hall of Titius Justus, where they sat and listened to teaching on righteousness, justification, law and grace, baptism, the Holy Spirit and much else, soaking themselves in the basic doctrines of the faith. One of the things that Priscilla particularly enjoyed was that there was no segregation here. The women were as welcome as the men! This was revolutionary to a Jewish woman, and she absorbed the teaching like a sponge. In fact, she became so well informed that she grew quite adept at actually explaining some of the teaching to others.

Not surprisingly, the rise of this ever-enlarging group did not pass without comment. The Jews were particularly wrathful and targeted Paul for trouble. At one point, they provoked a riot and brought him before the proconsul, Gallio; the Roman, however, was impatient with what he perceived to be mere controversy about their petty laws. Nevertheless, not long after that incident, Paul thought it would be prudent to move on. It was time to make a trip back to Jerusalem!

One night, he sat down with Priscilla and Aquila and outlined his plans. He would go by sea to Ephesus and from there to Caesarea and on down to Jerusalem. Then he drew a deep breath and looked each of them in the eye.

"Will you come too?" he asked simply. "At least, as far as Ephesus?"

"Why?" asked Aquila.

Paul smiled. "Things are going fairly well here, the church is established, and I think I can trust them to carry on now. I need to get back to Jerusalem and report to the brothers there. But I want to go via Ephesus and leave a Christian presence there. We haven't been there yet and it is a strategic city. I can't afford to spend much time there until next year, but you could stay and prepare the way. No one knows the basics of the Christian doctrines better than you two. And you are gifted in hospitality. You could establish a little community that we could later build on."

Aquila looked at his wife. She didn't know what to say

and dropped her eyes. Being a straightforward man, he answered cautiously: "I think we could do that."

"Good!" said Paul cheerfully, seemingly unaware of the host of radical changes he had just introduced into their lives.

All sorts of emotions were churning around in Priscilla. After the chaos of leaving Rome, their lives were orderly, their business was prosperous, and they were in the centre of a growing Christian community. It would be hard to leave. There were other considerations too. What about language? Customs? Ephesus was in Asia Minor.[2] True, it was very Romanized, but it surely would be different from Corinth!

And yet, she could not escape Paul's logic: Ephesus needed Christians, and she and Aquila were more mobile than most. Tent-making was fairly simple to set up anywhere, and they didn't have a young family to complicate things. They knew the foundational doctrines and could communicate them well.

But it wasn't just logic, was it? Paul always asked the Holy Spirit to guide him step by step. Only recently, he had told them of a vision he had had during a particularly stressful time, in which Jesus had spoken to him and reassured him, telling him to keep on preaching, for many people in the city were going to believe the gospel. Being a Christian was not just about doctrine; it was also about a devoted love relationship with the Lord. What did *he* want them to do?

A few weeks later, she and Aquila found themselves on a boat once more, heading across the Aegean Sea. When

2 Present-day Turkey.

they landed at Ephesus, Paul stayed long enough to go to the local synagogue and preach. He stirred up interest and promised to return. Then he left for Caesarea.

Ephesus

Aquila and Priscilla were now Christian missionaries to Ephesus. What should they do first? They set up their business to generate some income and establish themselves non-threateningly as part of the scenery. Also, following Paul's example as he had trained them, they went to the synagogue. This was the natural gathering place for Jews and a place where religion would be discussed, and so they could begin to put forth new ideas. But Aquila was not gifted in preaching like Paul, and Priscilla, as a female, was not permitted to utter a word in the synagogue, where strict segregation was observed and women were confined behind a lattice.

It was not easy for the couple to go back to the confines of Judaic meetings after the freedom they had learned in the church in Corinth. Priscilla could not sit with Aquila, nor pray out loud, nor prophesy. It was a matter of being willing to conform in order to win some souls for Christ. How could they make a breakthrough, to begin to communicate the good news of Jesus? Their prayers were answered unexpectedly.

A stir was caused one Sabbath when a striking young Egyptian from Alexandria strode in, evidently a "God-fearer". He was asked to address the congregation, and it was soon evident that here was an accomplished orator. Priscilla was astonished to hear him talking about John the Baptist, describing him as the forerunner and herald of Jesus. But, as she listened carefully, she knew this young man's understanding was not complete.

At the end of the meeting, she hurried over to Aquila and suggested they invite the stranger home for dinner. So Apollos came home with them. Priscilla and Aquila sat down with him and spent the rest of the day filling in the gaps. Apollos had been convinced of the authenticity of John's baptism of repentance, but knew nothing of Jesus' death on the cross as a substitute for sin, his resurrection, and the outpouring of the Holy Spirit.

With joy they explained the good news, and with great joy he received it. They met with him repeatedly after that, and wisely and lovingly grounded him thoroughly in Christian truth. Many a conversation was held around their dining table as they explained about law and grace, sanctification, and many aspects of Christian behaviour.[3]

Apollos had a brilliant mind and was a quick learner. He was also a gifted preacher. Now they had a champion in the synagogue who could preach powerfully! People began to be saved and the Christian community began to take root and grow, with Aquila and Priscilla at the heart of it, using their home for the embryonic church to meet in. But Apollos had not intended to stay at Ephesus indefinitely, and had plans to go across to Achaia in Greece. Now that he was a Christian, he had ready-made links in cities where there were churches. Priscilla and Aquila wrote letters to these other Christian communities, wholeheartedly endorsing Apollos as a powerful preacher,

---

3 At some point, Apollos would have been baptized (perhaps by Aquila?) and filled with the Holy Spirit.

a man greatly used by the Lord to strengthen churches and debate with opponents.

The little community in Ephesus was not left long without powerful leadership, because Paul came back. He had barely arrived when he ran into a group of twelve men who were in the same position that Apollos had been in; that is, they knew about John the Baptist but nothing else of Christian doctrine. So Paul explained the gospel to them, and they were baptized. Then he laid hands on them to receive the Holy Spirit. No doubt they were added to the existing company which met in the home of Aquila and Priscilla; their ability to explain the faith became a great asset to the church in discipling new believers, and their home a centre for hospitality.

History began to repeat itself, for after three months, opposition reared up again among the Jews, whereupon Paul left the synagogue and hired a hall belonging to a man named Tyrannus, where he gave daily teaching. Tyrannus let him have the place at a reduced rent, because Paul used it in the heat of the day when the rest of the citizens of Ephesus were indulging in a siesta.

This went on for two remarkable years. Paul not only preached, but also cast out demons. "Extraordinary miracles" happened when he laid hands on people. The whole region was shaken, as hundreds of people were saved. Paul's team of church planters was kept busy in training and discipling new converts, both men and women. Paul himself trained preachers and teachers, pastors and evangelists, his partners in the gospel.

These were happy, fruitful days for Priscilla. She liked living in this sophisticated city, with its paved streets, marble statues, its shops and baths and beautiful library. People flocked here from all around the Mediterranean to marvel at the awesome temple to the goddess Artemis with its soaring columns set in double rows. Nevertheless, many who came to marvel at Artemis's shrine became worshippers of Jesus as his good news was proclaimed everywhere.

Congregations of Christians were multiplying all over Ephesus, but the original group continued to meet in Priscilla's house (see 1 Corinthians 16:19). Her gift for hospitality, a key ingredient in church-planting, had plenty of scope! Also her gift for teaching was a great asset, and surely, later on when Paul wrote an epistle to one of his partners in the gospel, Titus, he must have had her in mind as he exhorted older women to teach the younger. Now a veteran of church-planting in two major cities, Priscilla was experienced in mentoring new Christians as they grappled with the implications of living godly lives in pagan societies.

Also, in a city heaving with the lascivious worship of Artemis, the example of a strong, loving Christian marriage had its own impact. She and Aquila had been married for many years now. For the last five or six, they had been Christians. They worked together in the tent-making business, they generously shared their home, they mentored new believers together, and, as leaders in the emerging Ephesian church, they gained respect because of their stability and faithfulness in a fickle and depraved environment. It required moral courage and commitment to swim against the prevailing currents.

But Priscilla also displayed heroic courage when she risked her life to save Paul's.

In that pagan culture there was bound to be intense opposition to the Christian message and it came when the silversmiths claimed that their trade in statues of the goddess Artemis was threatened, as people were forsaking her shrines and turning to worship Jesus.[4]

One afternoon, as Priscilla was returning from the hall of Tyrannus, she became conscious of a distant roaring sound. She stood still with her head on one side, listening intently. The roaring increased and became defined as excited shouting. As she hesitated, she realized that not only was it getting louder but she could also now hear angry phrases, and the drum of running feet. Then she saw Trophimus and Secundus heading toward her.

"Thank God you're safe!" they panted. They grabbed her by the elbows and whisked her along, back the way they had come, not pausing to explain until they reached the shelter of her own gate.

As her servant unlocked it and let them in, they told her that a riot was building up, escalated by a silversmith called Demetrius. He had called together all the workers of similar occupations in the *agora* (marketplace) and made an inflammatory speech in which he named Paul as responsible for endangering their trade. The workers, who made silver shrines to Artemis, became enraged and were baying for blood. The noise that Priscilla had heard was

4 Paul wrote to the church at Rome, commending Priscilla and Aquila, "who for my life risked their own necks" (Romans 16:3–4). We can only speculate but it is likely that it was in Ephesus during the riot, since they were all in Ephesus at the same time, a time of particular danger. This incident is imaginary, but I have tried to include the biblical ingredients: the risk that Priscilla and Aquila undertook was initiated by them; it was to save Paul; it was real danger, for they "risked their necks", so it wasn't a trivial event, but something quite severe.

their chant, "Great is Artemis of the Ephesians!" as they surged from the *agora* into the vast, open theatre.

"They've got Gaius and Aristarchus!" Trophimus said anxiously.

Secundus looked grim. "They'll be lucky to get out of there alive!"

"Where's Paul?" asked Priscilla worriedly. "He's the most at risk."

"We thought he was here – that's why we were running to your house!" they exclaimed.

Agitatedly, they looked at one another. Where could Paul be? Knowing him, if he got wind of what was going on, he would wade into the mêlée and be torn limb from limb!

"I just came from Tyrannus's hall," Priscilla said, thinking aloud. "He was still there then."

"So he could have left and got swept up in the crowd!" Trophimus wailed, despairingly.

"Or still be there," said Priscilla. "Look, if I run back now, I could get to him and warn him to come back here through the back alleyways."

The two men were hesitant to allow her to put herself into danger, so they went with her, back out into the narrow street that joined the main thoroughfare. But on the main street, all was confusion, and they became separated. The majority of the crowd had arrived in the theatre by now and were chanting and shouting, but on the streets there were still crowds, clamouring, arguing, pushing and shoving.

Priscilla, being smaller and lighter than the men, managed to wriggle through and make her way by back streets to Tyrannus's hall. The door was open, and Paul and Tychicus were just about to leave, Tychicus holding the key in his hand. There was an excited little knot of people around them, evidently trying to persuade Paul not to go to the theatre.

"But I must!" she heard him say. "It's me they're after, and it's on my account that this riot has been started. Maybe I can address the crowd and bring some sense to the situation."

Priscilla added her pleas. "No, no, Paul, don't go!" she pleaded. "The streets are full of crazy people who are in no mood to listen to anyone. If they see you, they'll kill you!"

"Prisca, I'm not afraid of death," said Paul gently, using his affectionate nickname for her.

But Priscilla was sobbing. "We don't want you to die yet, Paul. What would we do without you?"

Trophimus and Secundus appeared, panting. They had heard that a band of ruffians had been dispatched to look for Paul and bring him back to the theatre. The crowd was growing impatient. They were demanding to know the whereabouts of this fellow Paul who threatened their livelihood: "Bring him here, we'll deal with him!"

Suddenly, down the street they came, brandishing clubs and sticks. The circle of Christians was momentarily frozen, except for the quick-thinking Priscilla. "Paul, quick, we're about the same height – take my cloak, and I'll take your top tunic. I can head them off."

Even as she spoke, she had stripped off her outer cloak and hood, distinctively feminine in its colour and soft cloth, and grabbed at his top coat. There was no time to stand and discuss it; other hands tore off his garment and covered him in hers. She put on his, with the hood shadowing her features. Paul was suddenly transformed into a short, female figure and thrust to the back of the group with some tall men around him. Priscilla bent and rubbed some dirt onto her chin, the best she could do to improvise stubble growth.

The exchange was just completed when the gang accosted them. "Where's Paul?" they demanded roughly, "Which one is he?"

Priscilla dodged them and took off down the street at a run. Instinctively, the mob followed the fleeing figure, a short man in a rough brown cloak. She could not outrun them for long and when they caught up with her, they dragged her up the street with cries of triumph.

Meanwhile, Paul's friends hustled him down a side street into hiding, where he remained for a few days, protesting, but grateful for their loving protection.

Priscilla was swept along to the theatre, where confusion reigned. The vast arena was filled with thousands of frantic people. Some were shouting one thing, some another, and half of them had no idea why they were there at all! Rough hands shoved Priscilla onto the stage at the front where Demetrius was ranting.

"Here's your Paul!" someone shouted to him.

Demetrius broke off, and with a gleeful grin, rushed to grab "Paul" by the wrist. He was about to introduce him to the crowd, when a lone voice suddenly shouted, "That's not Paul! That's my wife!" and Aquila sprinted up onto the platform.

Never had the trembling Priscilla been more glad to see her beloved husband.

Demetrius pulled the hood back and Priscilla's hair came tumbling down, revealing that she was indeed not Paul, but a woman. Demetrius was incandescent with fury as the crowd laughed and yelled abuse. "*Who are these people?*" he hissed to his cronies.

A man named Alexander was thrust forward. He knew them, he said. The crowd was quieter, straining to hear and understand what was going on. This was a good moment, Alexander thought, to try and bring some sanity to the situation. He motioned with his hand. "Good Ephesians! I know these people."

Demetrius interrupted. "How do you know them?" he demanded rudely.

"They used to attend the same synagogue ..." Alexander began, but was shouted down by renewed shouts and catcalls.

"He's a dirty Jew!"

"Get him out of here!"

The uproar resumed with vigour for two hours, until the town clerk arrived and managed to restrain the crowd's emotions, and clear the arena.

Meanwhile, Priscilla was holding tightly to Aquila. They tried to slip away unobtrusively, but Demetrius shouted to a couple of his thugs who held them tightly. "Not so fast! You may not be Paul, but you *are* Jews and you deserve a thrashing. And you can probably tell us where Paul is."

One of his cronies added, "Jews? They're worse than that – they're ex-Jews, they're Christians!"

Demetrius's gang forced them out of the arena and down dark and twisting alleys. Priscilla shivered with fear, glad that Aquila was with her, but both of them knew that this could be the end for them. They were thrust into a dank, cold chamber and there the hours of endless taunts and cruelty began.

"'Jesus people'! A crucified god! What kind of a god is that? Start calling on Artemis to save you!"

Then the beatings began, interspersed with relentless questions about Paul's whereabouts. Wearily, Priscilla and Aquila stated truthfully, again and again, that they didn't know where he was. There was no opportunity to talk together on their own, but each knew the other would remain steadfast – faithful to the point of death, if need be.

Afterwards, Priscilla could not remember when it happened but suddenly in her pain and despair, she remembered Paul's and Silas's experience of prison in Philippi. After a vicious flogging, their backs covered in bleeding furrows, the two apostles had been chained to wooden stocks. In their utter humiliation, weakness and agony, they had made a strange decision: they would sing praises to God, right there. Their voices were weak and wobbly, and the effort took all their remaining strength, but they did it.

Resolve entered Priscilla's tired heart and body: she would do it too! Jesus had promised he would never leave her, so he was with them, even here. Love rose in her heart as, in a thin, quavering voice, she began to sing. Another voice joined in: Aquila's. There was an astonished silence for a few seconds, then yells of "Stop that!" from their tormentors, and one man landed a blow on Priscilla's head that nearly stunned her. Feebly, she and Aquila carried on, as the brutal beatings rained down on them. Priscilla could only recall the amazing presence of the Lord, as if he also was bearing the pain with them and giving them strength to endure.

Eventually, Demetrius turned up and called his dogs off. They untied the courageous couple, forced them limping along the street and left them huddled in a doorway. There they were found the next morning by some of their Christian brothers who had been searching for them.

The church received them back among them with great joy. Priscilla and Aquila, thankful to be with friends again, gratefully submitted to their loving ministrations as they tenderly cared for their wounds and nursed them back to health. Lying on her bed, Priscilla recalled her ordeal, but could find no bitterness in her heart. She was glad that she had been counted worthy to suffer for the name of Jesus and to follow him in this. As he had said, "Greater love has no one than this, that one lay down his life for his friends" (John 15:13). She was glad that she and Aquila had risked their lives for Paul; truly, if he had landed in the clutches of the enraged mob, he would not be alive now.

Paul and his leadership team prayed and talked together, and it was decided that Paul should leave, so he went north to Macedonia, taking some of them with him, to visit and strengthen the churches throughout Greece and Macedonia. They also talked and prayed about Priscilla and Aquila. After their beating, it would do them good to go by sea to another location. More especially, they would be an asset wherever they went. But where could such a valuable couple best be deployed?

How about Rome? There was a growing community of Christians there, in great need of teachers. The hostility against the Jews, which ebbed and flowed, had abated for the time being. *Rome!* Priscilla's heart leapt. She had always carried a secret place in her heart for the city she had grown up in and left so precipitately.

Rome

Soon they were off again, leaving their villa in Ephesus, their successful tent-making business and all their Christian friends. Priscilla had learned by now that it is foolish to cling to anything in this life, since this world, with all its undoubted pleasures as well as its burdens, is passing. She had another identity to add to her collection, that of a pilgrim.

She smiled as she waved at the receding group of friends on the Ephesian quay. *I may not be a mother,* she thought, *but I am a wife, a businesswoman, a teacher, a church planter. Now I am a pilgrim too. I am a citizen of another country, the kingdom of God. Last time I was in Rome, that was not true of me. I went away empty, a refugee. I go back full and enriched, to share with my brothers and sisters in Christ there.*

***

At the end of his epic epistle to the Romans, probably written around AD 56, Paul particularly sent greetings to his dear friends and fellow-workers "Prisca and Aquila ... who for my life risked their own necks" and to the church which met in their home. So he knew that they were once again using their gifts to bless and build up the saints: their home and hospitality, their teaching and mentoring, their example of a loving and faithful marriage, as well as a stable and fruitful business partnership.

Ephesus again

It would not have been surprising if, having made the full circle from Rome and back again, Priscilla and Aquila ended their days in that city. But we know they had one more term of service in them, for some years later, probably in AD 66, Paul wrote to Timothy who was in Ephesus at the time, and sent greetings to "Prisca and Aquila", his old friends. So when did they go back to Ephesus? Who knows? But no wonder Paul wrote affectionately that not only did he give thanks to them, but so did "all the churches of the Gentiles" (Romans 16:3).

Twenty years earlier, as Priscilla had boarded that boat with a heavy heart, a refugee fleeing from her home and all that was familiar, and taking to the open sea, she had had no concept of the adventurous life ahead of her. She had met the risen Lord Jesus and become his ardent follower; she had played a major part in building the church in three significant cities in three nations; she was taught by no less than the apostle Paul, who also regarded her as a beloved fellow-worker; she mentored Apollos, who became a mighty preacher; she helped establish churches which met in her house in different cultural settings. She may not have been a biological mother but she had spiritually mothered many young Christians. She had put herself in great danger on at least one occasion for the sake of Paul and the gospel. She was valiant and faithful, warm and hospitable, generous and outgoing, a Christian woman to admire and emulate.

Questions for group discussion

- **What do you think are the qualities of a pioneer?**
- **How do you think the marriage of Priscilla and Aquila benefited the churches they served in?**
- **How can mentoring be conducted in churches in the present day?**
- **Priscilla "risked her life" for Paul. What sort of dangers might pioneering women encounter today?**

CHAPTER 6

Mothers and Grandmothers

> *I am mindful of the sincere faith within you, which first dwelt in your grandmother Lois, and your mother Eunice, and I am sure that it is in you as well.*
>
> 2 Timothy 1:5

A crowd had gathered in the marketplace in Lystra, and curious to see what was happening, Timothy stopped and joined them. They were listening to a short-bearded man, speaking in an unfamiliar accent, accompanied by a taller man. Timothy realized that they must be the strangers who had preached in the synagogue the day before. His grandmother and mother had come home in an unusual state of excitement. They had told him that one of the strangers had brought a new teaching about a man called Jesus of Nazareth, who, he claimed, had been crucified, but had come back to life. "God has made Him both Lord and Christ – this Jesus ..." (Acts 2:36). His mother and grandmother, sensible, thoughtful women, had been convinced that the stranger spoke the truth.

Now here were these men again, preaching, so Timothy listened intently. The shorter one was speaking forcefully and eloquently, and the crowd grew bigger. Timothy noticed that a crippled man, whom he had often seen before, was sitting on the ground. Suddenly the preacher pointed at the man, and in a loud voice commanded, "Stand up straight on your feet!"

Timothy watched transfixed as the crippled man staggered to his feet, stood swaying uncertainly for a minute or two, then, with a look of utter incredulity on his face, began to walk. Next he began to jump up and down, and finally took off down the road at a steady trot and circled back. The crowd was silent with astonishment for a few seconds and then pandemonium broke out.

People began to shout and gesticulate. One cry was heard above the rest of the noise: "The gods have visited us!"

"Yes! Yes!" Others took up the cry. "The gods have come!" Some ran along the street shouting, "Zeus and Hermes are with us!" They ran to the temple and up the steps, looking for the priest. Frenzied excitement seized the crowd, and they surged forward, carrying the two speakers along with them. All were now shouting, "Zeus and Hermes are with us!"

As they arrived in the square in front of the temple, the priest came out and stood at the top of the steps. The crowd fell back, leaving Paul and Barnabas in the centre of a wide semicircle. Motioning with his hand, the priest called for silence. Some of the people were by now on bended knee. From the gloomy interior of the temple came two acolytes carrying garlands. As they descended the steps, they were followed by a third, who was leading a young bullock. The acolytes came towards Paul and Barnabas, and threw the garlands over their heads. There was a flash of steel as the priest raised a knife. He was about to plunge it into the heart of the bullock when both Paul and Barnabas, shouted in horror, "No! No! We are not gods! We are mere mortals like yourselves! We beseech you to turn from these things and worship the true God we have come here to tell you about!"

The crowd was reluctant to be deprived of its moment of excitement and celebration. A mighty miracle had been performed and their only explanation was an intervention by the gods. They were not disposed to listen to any other reasoning, even though Paul and Barnabas tore their clothes and ran from one person to the next, trying to persuade them that it was not they but Jesus of Nazareth who had healed the man.

Then another voice rang out. A group of men had mounted the steps, the very same who had already caused trouble for the two apostles in Iconium. Now they began to yell abusive and slanderous things against them. The fickle crowd became disposed to believe these newcomers, and started to turn on Paul as the main speaker. Timothy saw with horror that many were picking up stones and rocks, and hurling them at Paul. He put up his hands to defend himself, but a rock caught him on the side of his head and he sank to the ground.

Jeering triumphantly, the ringleaders dragged Paul through the dust, flung him outside the gate of the city, and left him there. The crowd quickly dispersed, but a little group of people who had believed Paul's message ran to his inert form. Timothy ran too, and joined them as they gathered around him. Barnabas was kneeling by his friend, tears pouring down his face, and Timothy heard him praying, "Oh, Jesus, Jesus, save him! Raise him up!"

Paul's eyelids fluttered and he sat up shakily.

Seeing him sitting there dishevelled in the dust, rubbing his sore head, Timothy's heart went out to Paul. He was bruised and concussed, but after a little while he stood up and insisted that he was all right, he would go back into the city. "I must preach the gospel in the next town," he said. Willing hands supported him, and helped him and Barnabas back to their lodgings.

Timothy walked home slowly, reflecting on all he had heard and seen. His mother met him at the door. She had heard the commotion and had been waiting anxiously. Glad that he was unharmed, she drew him in, shut the door and listened as he told her and Lois, his grandmother, everything.

The two women looked at each other, unable to conceal their excitement, as he told them of the healing of the crippled man, and of how the two missionaries refused to receive worship. "They said worship belongs to God alone, and that Jesus of Nazareth is God."

"Yes, we believe that too," they said, and explained again what had happened to them as they heard Paul preach. Timothy bowed his head. What a message of hope! And he had witnessed with his own eyes a miracle of healing that surely only God could do! He had also been deeply affected by the conduct of the two men who carried the message. They had preached boldly and brought healing to the cripple, but had resisted the adulation of the crowd to the point of being beaten up. Then, after all the abuse they had received, they had walked back into the city, determined to carry on taking their message elsewhere. Surely, what they preached must be genuine! The Jesus whom they preached must be wonderful if he was worth risking their lives for.

Paul and Barnabas left the next day and preached the gospel in Derbe. Then they returned to Lystra, and strengthened and encouraged the new believers. Now Timothy also opened his heart and committed himself to becoming a Christian. Paul and Barnabas appointed elders, and after praying tenderly for the embryonic church, they said farewell and returned to the city of Antioch from which they had come.

On their next visit to Ephesus some four or five years later, they found a healthy church. Among them was a young man "well spoken of by the brethren who were in Lystra and Iconium" (Acts 16:2). This was Timothy. Evidently, he had made rapid progress as a young Christian and was respected, not only in his own church in Lystra, but also among the believers in neighbouring Iconium. Not only that, it is clear from Paul's letters, written years later to Timothy, that Lois and Eunice were respected in the church for their "sincere faith". Eunice was a Jewish woman who had been married to a Greek Gentile. She must have taught Timothy the Judaic Scriptures in his childhood. Now, helped by Lois, they read the Scriptures and discussed their developing faith together. Her well-taught son now became a leading figure in the new church.

Paul saw that here was a young man with potential and gifting who could profit from close association with the apostle. Paul invited him to join his evangelistic team, and so began a deep and lasting bond with Timothy, whom he later called his "beloved son" in the Lord (2 Timothy 1:2).

But we are more concerned here with Timothy's mother Eunice and his grandmother Lois. How could they ever have foreseen that, simply by consistently loving and training young Timothy, they would earn a mention in the most read book in history? I feel that God allowed this to happen as a source of hope and encouragement to subsequent Christian mothers and grandmothers.

How many of us wish we could do something spectacular and courageous for God – something that would last, and earn us a place in history! But we are just mums and grandmas, and we spend our lives doing ordinary, humdrum things, like potty-training our children, teaching them how to hold a spoon and tie shoelaces, reading stories to them, meeting them at the school gate, helping them with their homework, and trying to train them to be kind, thoughtful, responsible human beings. Often it seems to be an uphill struggle. Our children disappoint us, exasperate us, even anger us at times. "Will they never learn?" we sigh, as we pick up their dirty socks for the umpteenth time, restrain them from hitting each other, and rebuke them when they answer back impudently. "If you hang up your coat/keys/bag where it belongs, you will always know where to find it!" we tell them. "If you tidy your room, you won't lose your library book." "If you *read* your library book, you might be able to do your assignment!"

We try to instil into them common sense, responsible attitudes to time and money, respect for authority, and loving obedience. It takes time, commitment and energy: things we are in danger of running out of very rapidly! We need help and encouragement, and I believe a major source of this is to know that what we are doing is important, effective and rewarding. The fact that Eunice and Lois are on record for training Timothy so well is proof that what we seek to do is of huge importance.

But notice that they are not mentioned merely for raising him well; they are remembered for passing on their faith. Paul affirmed that the same *faith* that was in them was subsequently found in Timothy. They both provided a godly example of *sincere* faith. This speaks of solid belief in God's word and a grasp of doctrine which motivated and undergirded them in consistent Christian living.

I am grateful that I observed this in my own mother. She never deviated in her love for the Lord, and it was his word which guided, shaped and motivated her whole life. This was also true of both my maternal and paternal grandmothers. Naturally, they were not perfect and had their quirks and failures; they belonged to their own generations, whose ways now seem quaint. Nevertheless, they lived in the light they had, praying for their children and grandchildren, and living out their lives based on Christian principles. This has been a priceless gift to me and I feel the weight of my Christian heritage.

By now, some may be thinking mournfully, *But I am the first of my family to be born again!* But be encouraged: as Christian women we have all been born into the worldwide family of God, and we "share in the inheritance of the saints in Light" (Colossians 1:12). All that Christ gained by his death and resurrection accrues to us! And every woman who becomes a Christian can be the beginning of a new chain of blessing as she prays for her family.

Praying for our families

How do we pray for our families? As a young mother, I began to search for scriptures that would give me some goals and direction. I found the Psalms to be a rich mine of treasure. Psalm 127:3–5 told me that my children could be like arrows in a quiver. The size of quivers varies; God knows what size our "quiver" is and gives us enough grace to carry it. Terry and I had thought that ours would carry four arrows, but to our surprise, God added a fifth! When we had got over the shock, we were thrilled that our quiver was being enlarged.

Arrows are straight, sharp weapons that are shot out from a bow with the intention of hitting a target; so we prayed that our children would each be sent out with a sense of direction, vigour and clarity, and that, wherever they went, they would do damage to the kingdom of darkness and bring glory to Jesus.

Psalm 144:12 says that our daughters are to be like "pillars carved to adorn a palace". This became a favourite verse of mine, as I meditated on various aspects of pillars. They need to be strong, straight and stable; they are supportive, indispensable to the structure of a palace or temple. And as they stand in orderly columns, with the light slanting on them, they add greatly to the beauty of a building. Some women may not feel that being a pillar is a very desirable ambition to have for a daughter, but if a mother prays for her to have some of those qualities, she will grow to be a strong, fulfilled woman and a great asset, both in her church and also to her future husband.

Terry and I used to read some Bible verses and pray

for our children at breakfast. One day, as I waved them off on their way to the bus stop, my heart ached, thinking that, as they left our front door and entered their schools, they were leaving one set of values to be bombarded by another. I went up to our bedroom and opened my Bible. I found my daily reading was in Isaiah 49. When I reached verses 24 and 25, I was excited and comforted.

> *Can plunder be taken from warriors,*
> *or captives rescued from the fierce?*
> *... this is what the LORD says:*
> *"Yes, captives will be taken from warriors,*
> *and plunder retrieved from the fierce;*
> *I will contend with those who contend with you,*
> *and your children I will save."*
>
> ISAIAH 49:24–25

So, even if the Enemy succeeds in taking captives, the Lord himself promises to fight on our behalf to rescue them! This was a huge encouragement, and became a powerful weapon in prayer, especially during periods when two of our sons were seduced by the Enemy's lies into backsliding for a while. God was faithful to his word and rescued them.

God's word reveals his desires for our children; as we use these scriptures in prayer, we are cooperating with him, declaring his revealed will. As a result, faith rises in our hearts, replacing fear.

How can we pass on our faith to our children? For one thing, it is good to let them know, right from the start, that our reasons for the way we train them are based soundly on the Bible. I wonder if Paul had Lois and Eunice in mind when he wrote to Titus and gave him some advice on how to relate to the women in his church: "Older women … are to encourage the young women …" (Titus 2:3–5). He follows this with six principles, including "to love their … children".

We find that the biblical way of loving is not a vague, wishy-washy, hit-and-miss affair based on how we feel at any given time. True love involves patience, clarity, and above all, consistency. The Bible has plenty to say about how to train children lovingly. Lois and Eunice were Jewish women and would have been conversant with the Old Testament. They would have known the verses in Deuteronomy, in the Psalms and in Proverbs that gave explicit instructions on how to train a child. It is likely that they were already training Timothy by these principles before they became Christians. Then, when they became believers in Jesus, their new faith added another dimension to their home life. If they had been motivated by the Law before, now they were motivated by the saving grace of Jesus!

Christian training should include clear demarcations of right and wrong, based on what is pleasing to God as defined in the Bible. But it should also be strong in teaching repentance and forgiveness, and in setting examples of these.

It seems likely that Timothy's father had died before Paul came to Lystra.[5] One hopes, however, that part of his

5 See John R. W. Stott, *The Message of Acts, The Bible Speaks Today* series, IVP, 1994, p. 254.

mother's and grandmother's training in faith included the ingredient of being secure in knowing *God* as his Father, because this is also foundational to faith.

As far as I know, the mention of Lois by Paul is the only reference in the New Testament to a grandmother. Now that I am a grandmother myself, it particularly interests me. Lois must have been saved fairly late in life: bearing in mind that by now Timothy was a young man, perhaps she was in her 60s or 70s. Sadly, as people get older, often their minds become less flexible, less open to new things. Therefore one must commend this elderly Jewish lady for her willingness to listen to the gospel with an open heart! It is a beautiful thing to see the humility of an older person whose mind is supple, and still eager to learn.

Attitudes towards older people are currently changing – or maybe it is simply that, as we get older, our definition of "old" stretches! When I was a child, I heard a preacher say, "As a young man of 34, I believe ..." My eleven-year-old mind was shocked. I thought 34 years old was ancient! Now of course, I think anyone aged 34 to be so young as to be barely responsible! Then again, a young friend who shares my birth date once asked me how old I was. At the time, he was eight and I was 55. He looked amazed when I told him my age: how was I still *breathing*? Now that I am in my 60s, it seems a long time since I was 55 – in fact, I was quite youthful then! So our attitudes change as we age.

Growing old gracefully

But this raises another question. In these days when cosmetic surgery is becoming commonplace, hormone replacement therapy is readily available, and face creams make unbelievable claims to rejuvenate the most leathery of skins, how should we, as Christian women, face growing old? Should we resist it or embrace it?

Behind a lot of the frantic efforts to retard the effects of age is fear: fear that we are no longer attractive or desirable, fear that we will become boring and lacking in zest and energy, fear of creeping inactivity and inertia, fear of being a burden to our families, fear of loneliness, fear, ultimately, of death. We cannot change our birth date, but at least we can shave a few years off the way we look!

As Christian women, we must not allow our lives to be dictated by fear. We know that we are more than an outward shell. God looks on our hearts; in fact, he has given us new hearts, new life, new focus, new desires. So, first of all, we must keep cultivating our relationship with him, and finding out what pleases him. However, that does not mean that we should not give attention to our bodies, to seek to keep them fit, properly fed and appropriately clothed. How much we spend on improving how we look is a personal issue, and varies according to individual taste and income. But I believe that Christian women can continue to glorify God in their bodies by looking after them, and continuing to celebrate their femininity right through old age, with style, colour and dignity.

I recall an elderly lady who came one day to our first little church in Seaford. She bought a house in the town and soon became one of our closest friends. She was in her 70s and had been a Christian for many years. At 40 years of age, she had married the love of her life. Three months later, he suddenly and unexpectedly died of a heart attack. I wept when she quietly confided this to me one day. It was very unusual for her to speak about herself; one of her main characteristics was to be more interested in other people.

I was a young mother of two when we met, with a two-year-old toddler and a new baby girl. Mrs Bendall became a dedicated babysitter and even moved house so that she could live across the street from us. She was gentle, selfless and full of fun, patient and loving with the children, and always supportive and prayerful. She had an amazing ability to communicate with any age group. There was a shy teenage boy in the church and I remember giving him a lift one day when Mrs Bendall was also in the car. In no time she put him at ease, by talking knowledgeably about the cricket scores.

I think one of the things that impressed me most about her was that her mind was open to God, and she was willing to examine new things that she had not previously been familiar with. So she quickly embraced the baptism in the Holy Spirit, and began to pray for prophecy and other spiritual gifts.

She became a little frail, and one day, concerned that she had not answered her phone, we managed to get into her house and found her dead on the bedroom floor. She had died of a heart attack in the night. She had been with us a few short years, but they were a priceless gift to us, especially to me. She modelled something to me that I shall never forget. Like the palm tree spoken of by the psalmist, she was "planted in the house of the Lord", still yielding fruit in old age (Psalm 92:12–14). She carried the sweet fragrance of Jesus with her, and her contentment and tranquillity, grown no doubt out of the soil of pain and grief, left an indelible impression on me.

We do not need to fear, as we get older, that we shall inevitably become trapped in old ways of thinking and be unable to embrace what God is saying to the church today. He is ageless, the "I Am", and he has put his eternal Spirit within us. As we follow him, and yield to him, we should find that we expand in his love and grow in wisdom. Mrs Bendall also taught me that we need older, more mature people in our congregations, and that they have much to contribute to church life. She would have been surprised, I think, at how highly we treasure her memory; she was not aware of how she enriched our lives simply by serving us lovingly and humbly.

However, Mrs Bendall had been a Christian for many years. How much greater the change for someone who becomes a Christian in later life, as Timothy's grandmother did! God comes to people of all ages, and it has been a delight in our church in Brighton to baptize new Christians from school age right through to old age. We need "grandma" figures in the church, whether they are biological grandmothers or simply dear, elderly ladies like Mrs Bendall, who can reassure and help tired young mums, and provide wisdom and understanding.

In the United Kingdom, in the current financial climate, it is often unavoidable for young mothers to work outside the home. Childcare becomes a problem, and increasingly, grandmothers are involved in helping to raise their grandchildren, often spending a lot of time with them. This can be a great opportunity for Christian grandmothers to pray for and influence the children, if they live nearby. But of course, in our increasingly mobile society, young women often do not live near their mothers, and yet cannot afford nursery care or are reluctant to entrust their children to child carers. Maybe this is an area where older Christian women can step in to help lift the load. (However, let us do all we can to encourage young mothers to understand the importance of their role and, if at all possible, to resist following the cultural norm of surrendering children to child carers. Much childcare is excellent, but a mother uniquely loves her child.)

Grandmothers must certainly not "write themselves off" in the mistaken belief that their days of usefulness are behind them. Their own children may not be walking closely with God, or they may be so tired and so busy that "Grandma" may provide the main source of spiritual nourishment to the next generation. I have many Christian friends who are grandmothers: they whip out a fistful of well-thumbed photographs at every opportunity, extolling the virtues and features of their little dears. As grandparents, we love to have our grandchildren come and visit, reliving the days when their parents were small. Our role is different now, of course: we do not have the final responsibility for the children, and our tolerance levels are usually higher than they were then. We think everything they do is wonderful. We love hearing of the funny things they do and say, we love the feel of them, the sound of them, the smell of them.

But our energy levels are lower than they once were, so it is also wonderful when they go home! The whirlwind that seemed to accompany them on their arrival recedes out of the front door, leaving the house quiet again. John

Wimber used to say, "If I had known having grandkids was this much fun, I would have had them first!"

However, we must bear in mind that our grandchildren are growing up in a harder world than the one we have known. They, like us, will have to negotiate the dangerous currents and whirlpools of a world full of terrorism, pluralism, materialism and secularism, but in their case the pressures will be more intense. Let us pray that they will also see the power of God more manifestly than we have, bringing millions of souls into the kingdom, demonstrating healing power, reconciling nations, and changing despairing societies into hope-filled communities. Not only that, we must pray that our grandchildren will be instrumental in bringing this about. Let us pray for our daughters and granddaughters to be like pillars adorning the house of God, and for our sons and grandsons to be warriors for God.

Every stage of life can be fruitful for the Christian woman. Some of us may be called into a public ministry. Most of us won't be, but God may give us a "Timothy" to pray for and nurture, someone who will one day be a mighty influence for God.

Questions for group discussion

- **How do you view your role as a mother? As a grandmother?**
- **How can we inspire our daughters to be like pillars in God's house?**
- **What scriptures help you to pray with faith for your sons and daughters?**
- **How can we keep bearing fruit for God, even into old age?**

CHAPTER 7

A Single Woman

I commend to you our sister Phoebe, who is a servant of the church which is at Cenchrea; that you receive her in the Lord in a manner worthy of the saints, and that you help her in whatever matter she may have need of you; for she herself has also been a helper of many, and of myself as well.

ROMANS 16:1–2

Phoebe. I wish Paul had said a little more about her! How old was she? Was she married? Why was she going to Rome? In what ways had she served the church in Cenchrea? And how had she been of help to Paul? How tantalizing these verses are!

It is difficult to picture her. Perhaps she was a middle-aged widow who had found her grieving heart comforted as she came to faith in Christ and became part of a loving community in the church in Cenchrea. Or was she an energetic young woman who had blessed the church with her prophetic ministry and was now on her way to help the church in Rome? Or maybe she was a dear, elderly saint who had poured her life into the Cenchrean church and now was visiting Rome, but was a little anxious about finding her way around.

There is no mention of an accompanying male, so I

don't picture Phoebe as married, at least not at this point. She may have been widowed, or never have married. There are few clues about her social status. Although this is a little frustrating, it is also reassuring, because Paul speaks of her with respect and affection regardless of her status.

What do we know about Phoebe for sure? She was a Gentile, and her Greek name means "pure". Paul spoke highly of her, using four words to describe her. These terms are also something of an indicator of how women should be perceived in a healthy church.

Women in a healthy church

The first was "sister". In 1 Timothy 5:2, Paul instructed Titus in how to relate to women in his church. He was to regard "older women as mothers, and the younger women as sisters, in all purity". Perhaps this indicates that Phoebe was not in the older category! Using the word "sister" helps us to understand something of the ethos of the early church and also how men and women should relate in our modern churches.

"Sister" implies a spiritual truth as well as a social attitude. It reminds us that we all belong in the family of God, whatever our status in the world. It helps us to esteem one another with dignity: each person has been saved by the precious blood of Christ, each is priceless to God, each has received God's grace in forgiveness and cleansing, each is the temple of the Holy Spirit.

The implications of this are worked out in our behaviour to one another. There is to be affection, esteem, friendship and respect, but there is no room for lust, immodesty or flirtatious behaviour. This is a helpful yardstick when teaching our young men and women how to conduct their friendships in the church. They can ask themselves: "Would I treat my sister/brother in such a way?" Paul's use of the word when describing Phoebe implies affection with respect, closeness with purity.

Secondly, he says she is a "servant of the church in Cenchrea". The Greek word for servant is *diakonos*, which has been transliterated into English as "deacon". This has come to be understood as a title for an official role in some denominations. We read in Acts 6 that seven men were set apart to take care of some practical issues, and they are often referred to as "deacons", although that appellation is not mentioned in that particular chapter. Later on, Paul spells out character qualifications for deacons in 1 Timothy 3, and here it would seem to imply that it was an office occupied by men. But given that the word means basically "servant", there must have been countless women who could be so described, and for whom the word was, and is, appropriate.

It may be that Phoebe had a definite function in the church in Cenchrea that was recognized by the label "deacon", or it may simply mean that she was a loyal, faithful, indispensable, hard worker. However, the fact that she is described by the male form of the word – that is, as "deacon" rather than as "deaconess" – is interesting.

In 1 Timothy 3:8–10, we find the qualifications set out for deacons. They were to be "men worthy of respect, sincere, not indulging in much wine, and not pursuing dishonest gain. They must hold the deep truths of the faith with a clear conscience". Then it goes on in verse

11, "In the same way, their [*gunaikos*] are to be women worthy of respect ..." The original Greek text does not include the word for "their"; the NIV inserts it. The NIV and the English Standard Version (ESV) translate *gunaikos* as "wives" but the word simply means "women". The following list of desirable qualities for these women mirrors that of the (male) deacons, and therefore some notable scholars interpret this verse as referring to women who had a diaconal role.[6]

Other references to godly women also support the possibility that some women were specifically recognized as functioning deaconesses. For example, 1 Timothy 5:3–16 is about the support and behaviour of widows. It could also imply that these widows were part of the administrative fabric of the local church and had to be of good repute. Certainly, later in church history, right up until the fourth century, there were women appointed with the title of deacon. In Phoebe's time, in the first century, this role may not have been so developed, but it appears that in Ephesus, at least, there were widows whose lives of prayer, hospitality and good works were recognized, and whom the church helped to support materially (1 Timothy 5:3–8).

It seems probable that deaconing had to do with acts of care and mercy, and so it would have been appropriate to have deacons of both sexes to minister to the needs of men and women. The reference in 1 Timothy speaks of older widows being eligible for help, using terms translated

6 For example, Chrysostom, Clement of Alexandria, Theodoret. See Sharon James, God's Design for Women: Study Guide, Clear Cut Media, 2008, p. 125.

as "on the list" (NIV) or "enrolled" (ESV), which could also be construed as being eligible to serve, as well as to receive help. So perhaps Phoebe was a widow, an older lady who had learned through personal suffering how to help others, one who had a sympathetic ear to listen to those struggling with life's hard knocks, who prayed with them and counselled them.

We might also note that it was in Cenchrea that Paul had his hair cut: perhaps her practical service extended to being the church hairdresser! Whatever her service consisted of, it was valuable and appreciated, and non-hierarchical. "Deacon" does not imply superiority or a position that sets the individual apart from the rest. In his epistles, Paul continually exhorts members of the churches to maintain a serving attitude to one another: "Through love serve one another" (Galatians 5:13); "Have this mind among yourselves, which is yours in Christ Jesus ... taking the form of a servant" (Philippians 2:5–7 ESV). Christians were not to seek high positions, but to outdo one another in loving service.

I instantly think of many women I know whose serving ministry is integral and indispensable to our churches: they work hard to make evangelistic events a success, welcome people on Sunday mornings, visit the ill and infirm, invite friends to meetings, pray for the sick, provide endless refreshments, cook and serve at weddings and Alpha course meals, give people lifts, pray, prophesy, and teach. These women are utterly indispensable and churches could not exist without them.

Paul totally endorses Phoebe, and goes on to ask the believers at Rome "to receive her in the Lord, in a manner worthy of the saints". She may have come from Cenchrea, but she is one of them! She is "in the Lord", a saint as they are.

"Saint", Paul's third description of Phoebe, is a good biblical word to describe believers. It is both an elevator and a leveller. All believers are elevated to be saints, which means "holy ones", those sanctified and set apart for God. At the same time, the word is a leveller because it gives no degree of preference. We are all saved by grace through faith in the sacrificial death of Jesus. There is no room for superiority or inferiority. Phoebe is to be received, not only because she is a sister and a servant, but also because she is worthy, as a saint.

The last word Paul uses to describe her is "helper": "she has been a great help to many" (Romans 16:2 NIV); "she has been a helper of many" (New King James Version). Actually, the Authorized King James Version calls her a "succourer" of many, and the ESV translates the word as "patron". The Greek word is *prostatis*, literally "one who stands before", a protector. This begins to give us a different view of Phoebe. If she was indeed a patroness of some kind, this would suggest that she was a woman of some substance, maybe lending credibility to the idea that she was a businesswoman, like Lydia (see Acts 16).

Romans 16:2 appears to be the only place where the word *prostatis* is used in the New Testament, so it is impossible to compare it with other parts of Scripture. That such a particular word was used could imply that Phoebe's help was of a specific nature, such as financial support, or protection from harassing authorities. So perhaps she was an influential citizen, and perhaps the help she gave Paul was to use her influence to speak up for him in some politically tense situation: the sort of woman who today could use her connections to procure a visa for someone seeking entrance to another country, or perhaps one whose influence could help secure the use of an auditorium for special meetings, or smooth the way through local council red tape!

So gradually, a hazy picture unfolds of a woman who appears to be single, possibly a widow; she is capable, possibly well known and influential, but with a compassionate, serving heart. She is travelling to Rome, so perhaps this is to do with business. The fact that Paul asks the saints there to look after her suggests that she is unfamiliar with that city. He himself has reason to be grateful to her, and so do many others, for she has been generous with her assets, be they wealth, position or connections, or all of these.

So what can we make of Phoebe? There is no Phoebe-shaped mould. She intrigues us because we know enough to realize that she was a valued and significant member of the early church, but not enough detail to fill out the picture very much. This gives us an opportunity to observe that women don't have to be married to be fruitful and appreciated; that a possibly rich woman can be a willing servant; that a woman may give help, but also need help; that a woman may be influential in the wider world, but also happy and humble enough to be regarded by her fellow-believers as a sister.

Women can be something of a barometer for the health of a church. In a healthy church they should have plenty of opportunities to use their gifts, and there should be a relaxed but mutually respectful attitude between them and the men. Where a church is dominated by men, the women can feel crushed and lose confidence. They will be ineffective and unfruitful, and their gifting will atrophy. Where there is a superabundance of strong women, or where the men are weak and uncertain, women can become strident and intimidating, and the men become passive and lacking in motivation.

Single women in the church

For whatever reason, many women in today's churches are single. Many are young, daughters of members who have grown up in the church, or possibly students, especially if the church is in a university town. Naturally, some will be unmarried women of differing ages, some divorced, some widowed.

We need to be sensitive to the needs of the single women among us, and not assume that, because they may not have a family to take care of, they are always available for odd jobs! We can be very thoughtless at times and treat them like wallpaper. I remember, years ago, the hurt of a close single friend who was, and is, deeply involved in church life. She was invited to the house of some friends one New Year's Eve, and gratefully accepted, as being on one's own at such a time is one of the pains of singleness. Imagine, then, the shock when she arrived to find the friends dressed to go out to a party, leaving her on her own to babysit! The fact that she often selflessly babysat, for them and for others, had led them to believe that it was all right to take her for granted on New Year's Eve!

We forget, too, that most single women among us are

holding down a job and looking after a house on their own. They have to shop, cook, and do the chores, maintain their cars, pay their taxes and insurance premiums – in short, deal with all the usual paraphernalia of ordinary life but without a partner to take some of the load. A single woman may not be up all night with crying babies and sick children (unless she is a lone parent), but she may be the only surviving relative caring for an aged family member. In addition, she has worries about health, money, relationships and lifestyle: she is not just "free" to jump into any gap where serving is required.

Many single women today are also mothers, and they are obviously hugely under pressure to care for a child or children, go out to work, and do all of the above ... without a husband! Coming into the family of God should bring them into a circle of friendship where they receive love, protection, encouragement and practical help. Sadly, many people perceive Christianity as "going to church" and therefore as one more thing to add to an already overcrowded life, when what it should mean is being embraced into the family that they were previously lacking, with all its attendant benefits.

Another huge area of pressure is the climate of sexuality which prevails, at least in the Western world. It is assumed these days that a woman on her own is looking for a sexual partner, either long-term or for only one night. For an unmarried young woman to maintain virginity, or for a single mother who is a Christian to remain celibate, is regarded as abnormal and unrealistic. In fact, such a woman is regarded as about as rare as an alien from another planet! It is especially hard for a woman who has lived a promiscuous lifestyle, or indeed has had a long-term sexual relationship, suddenly to change her habits when she becomes a Christian. This would have been no different for women in New Testament times, yet these are precisely the people whom Paul and the other apostles address in the early church, exhorting them to live "in all purity".

Many, many early Christian converts came out of totally pagan backgrounds with no clear moral values. Worship of various gods could involve orgiastic rituals. Slave girls would often have been used and abused by owners. Higher up the social chain in Greek society, there would have been no particular reason for a woman to be treated with respect unless she were the wife or sister of a very influential man. Mostly, females did not command respect in their own right.

So when women became followers of Jesus, Paul had to spell out the implications of the gospel. It was because they were now slaves of Christ that a new law prevailed: the law of love. Their hearts had been won by a new Master, whatever their age or status. They had new hearts and therefore a new inclination to please him and turn away from the old, empty lifestyle. This had implications for the use of their bodies, which were now the temples of the Holy Spirit and could be gloriously sanctified by him, and used for him. Instead of gratifying the lusts of the flesh, they could devote themselves to displaying Christ's love in deeds of kindness, loving service, and spiritual gifts such as hospitality, teaching, giving and healing.

The pressures on women were bad in those times; possibly, they are even worse today. People who maintain sexual purity are derided as "puritanical", "Victorian", "frigid", or simply as dinosaurs, their lifestyle a hangover from a sad past. If a woman does not sleep with a man, she is assumed to be a lesbian, although strangely, in our topsy-turvy world, that would be considered all right! It is being a virgin or celibate that is the problem!

Our so-called tolerant society is tolerant of any and every deviation, but it is increasingly intolerant of sexual purity. What used to be perceived as the "norm" is now abnormal, probably because it is seen as a threat to "freedom". Yet this "freedom" brings women into misery and further entrapment: broken relationships which cause broken hearts, unwanted pregnancies, family breakdown, disease, and a loss of security and identity. It is a lie. True freedom in Christ is the new God-given strength to live his way: to have the faith to believe that, though single, it is possible to live a happy, fulfilling life, to have true peace within, and to know that there is an inheritance awaiting those who love Jesus, which will far outweigh any fleeting pleasure on earth.

We live in a society which accepts that, if a woman is attracted to a man, it is natural to let that desire grow to the point where she will override other emotions and principles. To be "in love" is so applauded that being "swept off your feet" is regarded with approval. "We couldn't help ourselves," say the starry-eyed couple, but in the cold light of day the harsh realities of life intrude, when a baby is aborted, or when broken families struggle with the complexities of financial maintenance.

So what are we saying? That we should never fall in love? Women, married or single, all have a capacity to "fall in love". We have hormones; we respond to smiles, voices, songs, perfumes. It is not strange or wicked for a woman to be suddenly assailed by feelings of attraction for a man, but she does not have to be controlled by those feelings. Christians have, and can cultivate, the ability to recognize danger and pull back before it escalates into full-blown desire. It is not inevitable for them to allow that emotion, however pleasurable, to propel them into behaviour which leads to disaster. Contrary to popular opinion, it is not unhealthy to deny expression to that desire. Lust does not have to be slaked by indulgence. It can be refused.

Making choices, fighting battles

In the introduction to this book, I referred to some single lady missionaries who made the choice to stay single. Their choice was not a negative one which led them into a vacuum of life, devoid of love, appreciation or fruitfulness; it was a deliberate decision to refuse to marry a suitor because they had already committed themselves to a Master who called them to a specific way of life. It is doubtful if they could have achieved so much if they had married.

Non-Christians may try reason and willpower to deal with lust and temptation, if indeed they are motivated to do so. These weapons are often inadequate and impaired, but Christians have the mighty power of the Holy Spirit to help them make a choice that is glorifying to God. We can turn away, indeed "flee" from temptation, say "No", and "in the evil day ... stand firm" (Ephesians 6:13). We don't have to be overcome!

Often, the hardest part is actually to acknowledge the situation and verbally articulate it in prayer. We feel so bad, so silly, so weak and foolish confessing the truth and asking for help. But "if we walk in the Light, as He Himself is in the Light ... the blood of Jesus ... cleanses us from all sin" (1 John 1:7). Jesus knows the fights we have to engage in; incredibly, he had to fight them too, and because he did, and won, we can win. It is wonderful to be clean and have a clear conscience.

Single women in our churches are fighting battles, and we need to pray for them, befriend them, encourage and applaud them; they also need godly friends to whom they can be accountable. They are indispensable in the body of Christ, as indeed is every Christian, but perhaps one of their greatest callings is to be able to show a sceptical world that God really can bring peace, joy and fulfilment to a single person. It is not necessary to be married (or "shacked up") to be a complete person.

This brings us to another lie that must be exposed: that a man "completes" a woman. This implies that a woman without a man is only half a person, and *vice versa*. It is undoubtedly true that interaction with men can develop a woman's character and social skills, and that God uses all sorts of circumstances and people to grow us up and mature us. It is also true that Christian marriage is one of God's best tools for changing us. But let's be clear: no man can meet all of a woman's needs, much less complete her! Only Jesus can work in a woman (or man) to bring her (or him) to completion. God can, and does, bring together in marriage men and women who are very different from each other, but they don't "complete" each other; they bring complementary gifts into the relationship so that a unique partnership is formed.

God, however, is interested in transforming individuals, single or married, to become like him, so that the Father can look on them and say with delight, "This is My beloved ... in whom I am well-pleased" (Matthew 3:17).

The apostle Paul celebrated singleness. He suggested in 1 Corinthians 7 that to remain unmarried might cause a person to be more fruitful and effective. He treats the single state as being holy and healthy. Unfortunately, we often swallow the world's view that singleness implies rejection and inferiority. By this view, single women are missing out and living lives that are second best, while they mark time waiting for Mr Right to turn up! Nothing could be further from the biblical view of singleness.

A single woman needs to know that her heartfelt longings for a man are natural, that it is all right to pray for a husband, but that being married is not the only way to joy and fulfilment. (In fact, she has only to look around to see how many of her married sisters do not always exhibit such positive emotions.)

We often overlook the fact that the New Testament epistles were not written to individuals but to communities of believers. We have individualized Christianity in the West, forgetting that we need to support each other, be accountable to each other, look out for one another, pray for one another. A huge part of singleness is the sense of loneliness and isolation, but if we cultivated the sort of Christianity we see in the New Testament, a lot of that isolation would be alleviated. The church would become the context for sharing experiences of fun and laughter, pain and difficulty, anxieties about money, health, friends and relations, jobs, and fear of the future. Instead of coming home burdened with problems, with no one there to talk to about them, loving Christian friends could be the sounding board to help get things into perspective.

Phoebe was a woman who was obviously very fulfilled in her church activities and relationships. She was appreciated, recognized and honoured by Paul for her hard work. She was not a spectator; she played an active and vital role in the day-to-day function of the church. She was an integral part of the body.

One last thing: it is quite likely that Phoebe's visit to Rome provided the opportunity to carry Paul's letter to the church in Rome for him. If so, we may assume she arrived safely, for the letter has survived and blessed countless believers down the centuries, and I, for one, am grateful.

Questions for group discussion

- **How should Christian "brothers" and "sisters" behave towards one another?**
- **In what ways can single women serve their churches?**
- **How can we help the single women in our churches cope with the pressures of today's sexual climate?**
- **How can we help single women who long to be married?**

CHAPTER 8

A Businesswoman

A woman named Lydia, from the city of Thyatira, a seller of purple fabrics, was listening; and the Lord opened her heart to respond to the things spoken by Paul. And when she and her household had been baptized, she urged us, saying, "If you have judged me faithful to the Lord, come into my house and stay." And she prevailed upon us.

ACTS 16:14–15

She had everything money could buy. The villa on the hillside overlooking Philippi was even more spacious and opulent than her other home in Thyatira. Her business, inherited from her husband, was flourishing. After his untimely death, she had consulted his overseer who had worked with him for many years and knew the business inside out. She had listened carefully, asking pertinent questions, her astute mind quickly grasping principles and potential.

The balance sheet was healthy. There was constant demand for the luxurious purple cloth they made and marketed, and the widow calculated that the time was ripe to expand. She decided not to sell the business but to continue to run it and investigate possible new markets. Soon she had her merchants travelling into Macedonia.

Philippi, a Roman colony, and ever hungry for more purple cloth, became another centre of operations.

Lydia travelled there herself to supervise the establishment of this new base. She liked this elegant city by the river. It had been established as a Greek city by Philip of Macedon, but was now a Roman colony, cosmopolitan and cultured. Now a rich woman, she purchased land and built a large villa. She divided her time between Thyatira and Philippi, and enjoyed a luxurious lifestyle. But now, in her middle years, she was comfortable but lonely. There was an ache in her heart for companionship, but also for a sense of purpose in life.

One day as she was walking by the river, she met a group of women and entered into conversation with them. There was an air of solemnity and tranquillity about them that appealed to her, contrasting as it did with the materialistic, money-grabbing mindsets of merchants that she had become accustomed to. These women were Jewish and they began to speak of their faith in the God of the Judaic patriarchs.

Raised in Thyatira, in the old kingdom previously known as Lydia, she was used to the worship of capricious deities who always seemed to be angry, demanding and unpredictable. These gods offered no certainties on which one could base one's life, no explanations for life's problems. She craved clarity, answers, meaning. The Jewish God at least seemed consistent, and had given his people a system for their lives. She thought that maybe here, among these women, she could find friends and answers to her questions. Week by week, Lydia made her way to the river, usually accompanied by some of her servants, and after a while she adopted the God of Israel as her God. She could not become a Jew, but became a "God-fearer".

Then one day, a group of travel-stained men arrived and respectfully joined them. They were Jews also and explained that they had been looking for a synagogue, but not having found one, were searching for some Jews meeting in the area.[7] As was customary, the travellers were invited to speak.

Paul introduced himself and his companions, and explained that they were on a journey. He then went on to tell of a time when he himself had been on a journey from Jerusalem to Damascus. He was hunting down people whom he understood to be a threat to the Jewish way of life, followers of a rabbi named Jesus. The women listened attentively: here was a man who was well bred, orthodox, who understood the Scriptures and abhorred blasphemy! Paul particularly noticed an elegantly attired woman whose dark eyes were fixed on him with a burning intensity. He continued with his account of how he was suddenly struck down, as a light brighter than the noonday sun shone from heaven and a voice spoke to him: "Saul, why are you persecuting me?"

There was a dramatic pause. The eyes of all were riveted on him. Paul himself was visibly moved as he continued, explaining that this encounter was with Jesus of Nazareth, who had been crucified and buried but had risen from death on the third day. Paul believed Jesus to be the long-

7 To establish a synagogue, a quorum of ten men was required; presumably there were no male Jews, or fewer than ten, in Philippi, which was why the women had found another meeting place by the river.

awaited Messiah, the Son of God, the Creator of all things, and now Saviour and Lord. He alone could forgive sins and reconcile sinful people with God the Father.

His hearers were stunned. Some were indignant and called to their children, picked up their belongings and went home. Others stayed behind, talking in little groups, questioning Paul's companions, disposed to hear more. Paul watched as the elegant lady in the purple shawl made her way towards him. She extended her hand to him and said, "Sir, I would hear more of this! Something is persuading me that you are speaking the truth."

"What is your name?" he enquired.

"I am known as Lydia, as I am from that region," she responded. She waved her arm in the direction of her maids. "Those are my servants," she explained.

Paul perceived that God was opening her heart. He and Lydia went and sat on some rocks by the river, leaving her servants talking with Luke and Silas and Timothy. A torrent of questions poured out of her, but as the afternoon wore on, the torrent subsided as Lydia drank in the truth that Paul was communicating to her thirsty soul. This was what she had longed for. To know why she was created, who God was, how she could know him, how she could find forgiveness and peace for her restless heart.

At length, she exclaimed, "This is true! I do believe that Jesus is the Christ! I want to know him too."

Paul called to his friends, who had been earnestly discoursing with her servants. As they came together, Lydia could see that the same light was dawning in them too. Together they stood and Paul led them in prayer. They confessed their sins and declared their belief in Jesus as the

Son of God, receiving his mercy and forgiveness through his death on the cross. The sun was getting low in the sky as they went down into the river, where Paul and Silas baptized Lydia and her servants.

As they stood dripping on the bank, Lydia turned to the apostles with shining eyes. "You must come to my house!" she exclaimed. "Come and explain to the rest of my household!"

The travellers looked at each other. They were tired. A few days earlier, they had landed at Neapolis on the coast. This morning they had walked the ten miles up the Egnatian Way to Philippi, found the meeting place, preached the gospel, and talked with the Jewish women. Now this new convert was asking them to come and preach some more!

Looking at their tired faces, Lydia understood. "Oh, do come!" she insisted. "You can rest and have a meal at my house."

They had no other plans and the thought of a meal and a place to rest was enticing, so gratefully they agreed. Lydia sent two of her maids ahead to alert the household that guests were on the way.

As they followed her up the steep streets, the apostles had no idea what kind of house they would find. Eventually, they found themselves in a spacious area at the top end of the town. The gates of an imposing villa stood open, and Lydia led the way into a beautiful garden, past a pool and into the cool, marble interior of the atrium. Somewhat awestruck by their opulent surroundings, the weary travellers gratefully accepted Lydia's hospitality. As they enjoyed a good meal, she happily informed them that there was plenty of room for them to stay there.

Slightly wary, they looked at one another and then to Paul. Was this right, they wondered? They had laid down everything for the sake of preaching the gospel; they had not flinched at hardship, had been slandered and stoned, had slept rough, endured imprisonment, beatings, hunger and thirst. This magnificent villa, with all its comforts, was a welcome relief. And yet, wasn't it rather self-indulgent for followers of the One who had nowhere to lay his head?

Paul grinned at their anxious faces. "Well, this is better than the damp ship we were in a few nights ago! And I would rather have this than that flea-bitten inn where we stayed in Neapolis, not to mention being stoned in Lystra." He stretched out on the couch with its silken cushions, and went on reflectively, "Yes, I know what it is to be in need. Now I am learning to enjoy plenty. The secret, my brothers, is to be content in every situation, by drawing on God who strengthens us." He looked round at their relieved faces and smiled. "It's good of this woman to share her home. Now let's thank God for good food and safe, comfortable beds tonight. No doubt we shall find ourselves roughing it again before long!"

When Lydia retired to her own quarters later that night, she sat for a long time on the balcony under the stars. The sweet scent of jasmine floated up from the garden, and she could make out the dark silhouette of the encircling hills. Faint sounds came from the city spread out below, but here all was tranquil. She revelled in the peace that had taken possession of her since she had committed herself to Jesus of Nazareth, Son of God, earlier that afternoon. Since that moment, things had begun to fall into place; a sense of completeness and rest had come to her troubled mind. Now she only wanted to live for him who had poured out his love into her lonely, searching heart.

There would have to be radical changes, she knew that, but she would face them tomorrow. Tonight she would sleep in peace.

In the days that followed, a pattern began to be established. Paul and his friends would spend some time in prayer and discussion in the morning. Then they would troop off to the meeting place by the river and preach about Jesus, spending much of the day there, and return at night, exhausted but exhilarated, and hungry for the excellent meals that Lydia's staff provided.

But what difference did it make to Lydia? Now that she had become a Christian, her heart was at peace, but what about her money, her possessions, her lifestyle? She moved in cultured society; she answered to no one; money brings power and she had plenty.

She was from Thyatira, a city which was a centre of commerce, where every business had its guild. The butchers, bakers, traders in oil, marble, cloth – all belonged to a guild, each of which had its own traditions and rites associated with various gods and goddesses. Often, the festivals and feasts degenerated into wild, promiscuous orgies.

Lydia now had some hard thinking to do and some uncompromising decisions to make. If she said nothing about her recent conversion, and carried on as before, she would be compromising her new beliefs, going against her conscience, and denying her new Lord. If she decided she could no longer participate in rituals which were wanton and lascivious, she might find herself despised, cold-shouldered, ostracized, marginalized. Her business would suffer; she could even be ruined.[8]

Meanwhile, Paul and his friends had good cause to thank the Lord for the day when he opened Lydia's heart by the river, for not only were she and her household saved, but the villa provided a meeting place for the embryonic church. The crowd down by the river was growing daily, many people were becoming Christians, and it was difficult to know how to teach them and where they could assemble for instruction. Lydia's home was the obvious place: it was spacious and self-contained, and the growing group of Christians wouldn't have any trouble from an unsympathetic landlord!

Things seemed to be going well, until one day a young woman started causing a disturbance. She was a well-known figure in Philippi, a slave girl owned by two men, who had become very rich because of her extraordinary powers of predicting the future. She began to follow Paul and his companions shouting, "These men are servants of the Most High God!" It was something of a joke the first day, but when she did it day after day, they began to find it exasperating.

Finally, Paul had had enough. He turned round and faced the girl and spoke to the demon that was controlling her. "In the name of Jesus, I command you to come out of her!" he said firmly. Immediately, the demon left her, and with it her fortune-telling power. Naturally, her

8 Interestingly, it does not appear that Paul instructed Lydia to sell her house and give all the proceeds to the poor. Evidently, when she became a Christian, she relinquished her rights to her house; all her riches were laid at her new Master Jesus' feet, and her villa was his provision for what would become the Philippian church.

owners were furious as all their money-making potential disappeared, and they blamed Paul and Silas. They dragged the two apostles before the magistrates, accusing them of breaching the peace. A rioting crowd yelled their agreement, and Paul and Silas were flogged and thrown into jail without trial.

Now Paul's teaching on being content in whatever circumstances they found themselves was severely tested! With their backs raw and bleeding, and their feet manacled, the apostles took stock of the situation, and decided to be consistent. They began to sing praise to God. Sometime after midnight, there was a violent earthquake, and the foundations of the prison were shaken. Cell doors flew open, and chains fastened to walls that were now crumbling were loosened.

The jailer rushed in; seeing the damage, he despaired of ever finding any of the prisoners again. Certain that they must all have escaped, and that he would have to face the consequences, he grabbed his sword and was about to kill himself.

A shout from Paul restrained him. "Calm yourself! We are all here."

Relieved and amazed, the jailer threw himself at Paul's feet. These men lived life on a wholly different plane from his!

"Sirs, what must I do to be saved?" he demanded.

Before long, he and his household had turned to Christ and been baptized. Now they also were part of the church. What a diverse company this Philippian church was turning out to be! A rich woman and her servants, a slave girl set free from demonic powers, the jailer and his family, among others. They all met in Lydia's house to celebrate the release of Paul and Silas from prison, rejoicing in their salvation and their friendship.

***

These were remarkable days for the early church – and yet days in which real-life issues had to be faced. Lydia would have had to confront a number of issues. First, and most obviously, she was a woman. We don't see Paul telling her that because she was now a Christian woman she must stop operating her own business and become first and foremost a homemaker. The Bible says that Lydia pressed him and his companions to avail themselves of her house, and by the end of Acts 16, we read that the church was meeting there (verse 40). If Paul had been uneasy about her wealth or occupation, surely he would have deterred the church from profiting by it.

So Lydia was wealthy. Why did she not sell her house and land, and lay the proceeds at the feet of the apostles, as Barnabas had done (See Acts 4:36–37)? Or why did not Paul instruct her to give her wealth to the poor, as Jesus had told the rich young ruler? It appears that there is no one rule that fits all. Some are called to give up their riches and live in poverty, like C. T. Studd. He was a rich and famous young man in the late 19th century. When he inherited his father's wealth, he sat down with his young wife and wrote out a number of cheques to missions and charities. The couple disposed of his entire fortune and sailed to China as missionaries. Florence Nightingale was a wealthy young woman who gave up everything to serve sick people in terrible war conditions in Crimea. Some are called to use their wealth to make more to give away.

Others use what they have with overflowing generosity, and God can trust them because they do not have sticky fingers. In 1707, a girl was born into the family of an earl in England. She lived among the aristocracy, and at the age of 21 was married to the Earl of Huntingdon. After she lost four of her children and was severely ill herself she began to seek God. She became a Christian and developed friendships with John and Charles Wesley, and George Whitefield. She unhesitatingly used her wealth and influence to open doors for these men to preach and gave generously to congregations to build churches, many of which still stand and are in use today. In an age when women didn't have many opportunities to serve the Lord publicly, she used her money and position to spread the gospel. It is said that the king himself held her in high regard.

Besides wealth, Lydia would have faced the problems of operating honestly in a wheeler-dealer world, which is also true for many today. What does the Bible teach about the world of work? And especially about women at work?

God designed us to work

Work is something which God ordained from the beginning. God himself was at work in creation and found it very satisfying. Human beings, made in the image of God, were also intended to work, and to find it fulfilling and satisfying. God made a garden, then made a man, and gave him the job of caring for and developing the garden. Things looked even better when God made a woman to help him!

God created the universe to have structure and form and purpose. He made human beings in his image, like him, to bring about structure, order and purpose. Work is not intended to be futile and meaningless; it is about working with God to bring order out of chaos, fruitfulness out of barrenness, meaning out of futility. We were intended to work, and it should be a blessing, not a chore!

But when the man and woman got out of step with God, everything became dislocated. The ground itself became cursed, and work became sweated labour. People's hearts became tainted with sin, and so everything they did became polluted – with pride, avarice, selfish ambition, wrong thinking. Humanity lost sight of the glory of being co-workers together with God.

Then Jesus came and lived his perfect life, died his sacrificial death, and rose again so that we might be reconciled to the Father. This means that he is restoring all things, including a right way to think about and approach work. Becoming a Christian changes one's attitude to one's work. From now on, we regard ourselves as "His workmanship, created in Jesus Christ for good works" (Ephesians 2:10). Whatever we do, we are to do it with all our hearts as service and worship to him.

This applies to men and women, whether we are in paid work in a supermarket, a hospital, an office, a school, running a business, or working at home with the children. We must not only understand "work" as what people are paid to do outside the home. Mothers who choose to stay in the home to train and care for their children work very hard indeed.

If we run our own business as Lydia did, we must run it

with integrity, truthfully and responsibly, and caring for any workers we might employ. We will find satisfaction in our work as we regard whatever we do as being for the Lord.

We also need to work with faith: we will need faith if we stay in the home, faith for God's provision if we are relying on one limited income, faith for stamina, faith for patience, faith that we are obediently serving God while we clear up messes, toilet-train toddlers, deal with temper tantrums, and pour out our love and affection on these demanding little human beings!

We will also need faith if we are working in paid work outside the home: faith to be honest, to represent the King well, to trust him with our family, to help us get priorities right. Faith says, *God has given me this work. I will do it in such a way as to bring satisfaction to him. I will trust him that, as I am here by his appointment, he will look after the consequences of my actions*. There will always be challenges, and temptations to compromise.

Fear will try to reason along different lines: If I walk the right path here, I will be laughed at or misunderstood, or I risk losing business, or everything will collapse. If I don't attend such-and-such a club/festival/course, I will be sneered at; I will lose face as well as money. I will be seen as one of those weird Christians. No doubt Lydia faced similar challenges. It is not a new problem!

So we need faith if we choose to work in the home, just as we need faith to embark on a career. Faith comes by hearing what God wants us to do, and doing it.

Faith also brings peace of mind, because the consequences of doing God's will are his responsibility. A friend of mine whose husband is church-planting has three children and an extremely demanding and influential job in politics. Her agenda would make most people curl up and die! But she walks through her life with amazing tranquillity of mind, because she is convinced that God has called her. Therefore she does not need to manoeuvre and manipulate in the workplace: she trusts God to open doors for her. She knows she will be targeted for anger and abuse at times, which will be unpleasant, but it will all hit the shield of faith that protects her. God gives her wisdom to make good decisions that have the potential to make huge changes in society.

Similarly, one of my own sisters has an influential post, overseeing retirement and nursing homes in the southeast of England. (Her children are now adults with their own families.) Her husband leads a new church which was planted about five years ago. Their lives are extremely busy, but happy, as they seek to find God's priorities. Sue loves her job and finds it very fulfilling; she also loves the growing church they are serving, and she confided to me that, at times, she had wondered if she could do more "in the church". Then her husband told her that she must do what God has called her to do, which is to be an influential Christian in the workplace. The contacts she makes, the words she speaks and the money she earns are all useful to the Christian community. Let us note that there is no stereotype of "the leader's wife" in the New Testament.

Faith also believes that if we honour God, he will honour us. That does not necessarily mean everything will turn out happily ever after in this life, but it does mean a reward ultimately in eternity.

We don't really know whether Lydia was married or

not. She may never have married, or she may have been married with or without children when we meet her in Acts 16. But as there is no mention of a husband in the narrative, and given the difficulties of women taking initiatives on their own in those times, I have assumed that she was a widow of a businessman, but this may be completely erroneous.

Working wives

A principle that married Christian women need to consider is that God created Adam and gave him his work, and then brought Eve alongside to help him to do it. The principle here is that the woman is a helpmate for the husband. In other words, a wife should ask herself, "Is what I am doing helping my husband in the work God has given him? Or is it hindering him?" Every couple has its own capacity and mix of gifts. Some marriages will flourish where both husband and wife are working at high-powered jobs for which God has called and equipped them. Some marriages limp along when the wife could be working but won't, or the husband requires her to stay at home when she has the capacity to do both. Other women are born homemakers and happily give themselves to that alone. Husbands and wives need to consider the issue prayerfully together.

We are not called to live by rules, but by hearing the Shepherd's voice. Sometimes it is right for a woman to be confined to the home, sometimes right for her to be in the workplace. There are times and seasons, and we must learn to discern them.

Should a wife work outside the home? Most young

wives today would be amazed that we should even ask the question! Yet just a few decades ago, not many young women had full-time jobs outside their homes. Most today don't even have the choice because of the economic demands of the society we live in. But when children start arriving, it is a question that needs to be faced. The demands of juggling the welfare of the children with a job become a major concern: couples can go round in circles trying to work out what their priorities are. A young Christian wife may find it easier to make a decision if she fixes in her mind that her first calling is to help her husband; likewise, the husband is guided in his decision if he recognizes that his duty towards his wife is to lead her and love her in a sacrificial way, just as Christ loved the church.

We can apply these principles in whatever sphere we work. If we are at home with children most of the time, we can be very tempted to give in to feelings of frustration. We can discount what we do as having little value if we measure it by the world's standards. But if we look at it from God's perspective, we can see it as a huge responsibility, a great privilege and a challenge for which we need all his grace, patience and creativity.

Some may be thinking, *Lydia was her own boss. She was free to make decisions, go to different places, exercise creativity, and tell other people what to do. But I'm trapped. I'm in a dead-end job with no prospects; I can't fulfil my potential here!*

But we must remember that, wherever we are, we are designed to bear fruit for God. Writing to the Philippians, Paul says, "in the midst of a crooked and perverse generation ... appear as lights in the world" (Philippians 2:15). We can shine as lights in a dark world when we are illuminated by the truth that God is with us, giving us a different attitude and motivation.

There is a true story of a highly trained and cultured Chinese lady who was a surgeon. It came to light that she was a Christian. This immediately unleashed forces of opposition and she was challenged to deny her faith. She refused, even when threatened with demotion. Eventually, when it became apparent that she was implacably steadfast, she lost her job. The only occupation she was allowed was to clean the toilets.

How did she cope? She told someone that she cleaned every toilet as if she were preparing it for Jesus himself. In the world's eyes, she was totally humiliated; in heaven, she will be way up among the stars! Serving the Master in any capacity is acceptable worship to him.

Questions for group discussion

- **What kinds of hazards can a Christian woman encounter in the workplace today?**
- **How do you regard your work?**
- **Wealth brings status: what do you think about that as a Christian?**
- **What are the frustrations of a "stay at home" mum? What are the frustrations of a woman who works outside the home?**

CHAPTER 9

Charismatic Women

1 Corinthians 11 – 14; 1 Timothy 2:11–14

Corinth. Bustling, brimming with colourful life, a seaport and melting-pot of nations: from Italy to the west, Asia Minor to the east, Macedonia to the north, and Crete and North Africa to the south.

Paul and his team were working their way down the east coast of Greece, having preached the gospel in the major cities. Paul had arrived a little ahead of the others; as was his custom, he began by finding the synagogue, and was soon given an opportunity to preach there. At this stage in his travels he needed three things: friends, a place to stay and money. All three needs were met when he ran into a couple called Aquila and Priscilla. They were Jewish, extremely hospitable, and were also tent-makers by trade like him. Soon Paul was not only sharing the gospel with them, but sharing their home and working with them in their tent-making business.

Meanwhile, Silas and Timothy had lingered in Macedonia, probably to establish the new believers in Philippi. After a while, they too arrived in Corinth. Their arrival released Paul from his manual labour, and he turned to teaching and preaching, supported by a gift of money which Silas and Timothy had brought with them from the saints up the coast. Paul now "began devoting himself completely to the word, solemnly testifying ... that Jesus was the Christ" (Acts 18:5). The Jews, however, became openly hostile and abusive, so he left the synagogue and went to a new venue nearby. Some of the Jews who had become Christians left with him, notably Crispus, the leading rabbi, and his entire family.

Many other Corinthian citizens believed and were saved. Over the next 18 months, Paul worked hard, preaching, teaching, instructing new Christians, battling with critics and labouring to bring some shape and structure into this disparate group of people, drawn from a hugely ethnically mixed city. At one stage, feeling worn down with all the challenges, he was sustained by a vision in which Jesus appeared to him with words of encouragement: "Do not be afraid ... go on speaking ... for I have many people in this city" (Acts 18:9–10).

So what did this embryonic church look like? Who were these "many people"? We find some of the answers in the letters that Paul later wrote to the Corinthians. There were those for whom eating food previously offered to idols was a big hurdle, while this did not pose a problem to others. There were men and women from sordid backgrounds who were saved but still behaved immorally: Paul later had to address incest. Then, among all the seething cultural confusion, quarrelling broke out, and contenders were suing each other in the courts!

Mixed up in the cultural problems were gender issues. There were chaste Jewish matrons like Priscilla, but there were also Greek women from a totally pagan background whose previous worship of capricious and promiscuous gods and goddesses often involved sexual acts. Paul later wrote to the Corinthian church that the lifestyle of "the sexually immoral ... idolaters ... adulterers ... homosexual offenders ... thieves ... drunkards ... slanderers [and] swindlers" was not compatible with the rule and reign of Jesus. Yet, he went on: "that is what some of you were. But you were washed, you were sanctified, you were justified in the name of the Lord Jesus Christ" (1 Corinthians 6:9–11).

Paul had to teach the Corinthians a new principle, that their bodies were no longer their own, but the property of the Holy Spirit. Indeed, more than that, they were the temple, the dwelling place, of the Holy Spirit. Indwelt by him, they could no longer let fleshly appetites overrule their behaviour. Bodies were not to be indulged with overeating, excessive drinking, or with sex outside of marriage. The glorious truth was that bodies once given over indiscriminately to carnal appetites were now rescued and indwelt by the Holy Spirit. They must be regarded as holy and honourable, able to bring glory to God by submission to him.

In the church, then, were ex-prostitutes, ex-adulterers, ex-thieves, ex-everything! Probably, there were women from the brothels and taverns down at the docks, women who had been used in corrupt sexual activity in pagan temples, respectable Jewish women, merchants' wives and daughters, maybe African slaves, sophisticated Greeks from Athens: a melange of women who would never have met in any other context, but who were now all drawn together by their love for Jesus who had washed them in his blood, freed them from guilt, and filled them with peace and joy in the Holy Spirit.

A lively church

Imagine what a riot Sunday morning must have been! The only worship any of them had previously known was either depraved idol worship or the sedate, carefully segregated worship in a Jewish synagogue. Now that the Jews were free from the Law, they could cast off all previous restraints. Now that the Gentiles were free from their futile pagan fears and practices, they could allow their affections to be engaged, but with purity and purpose. The Holy Spirit filled them all with exuberant joy, which was often expressed using gifts of tongues. There were no rules, just saved people and the Holy Spirit.

It sounds wonderful – but risky!

Imagine: a man begins the service with prayer, but a prostitute, who was saved the day before, excitedly butts in, bursting to tell her experience of salvation. Thrilled by her story, someone enthusiastically speaks in tongues but, before an interpretation can be brought, others join in. Singing breaks out, and then eventually, an appointed elder attempts to give some systematic teaching, but is interrupted by a woman who is mystified and demands an explanation, much to the embarrassment of her husband. Then a young woman from the docks fervently prophesies, her head uncovered, which is deeply shocking to the Jewish women sitting decorously veiled at the back.

Lively but chaotic! The elders were at their wits' end. As they attempted to bring order into chaos, factions began to develop, some declaring that Apollos, a recently saved Egyptian from Alexandria mentored by Aquila and Priscilla, was their teacher, while others argued that only

Paul had authority. The ex-Jews were inclined to stick with Peter, while others, weary of controversy, declared they would follow no one but Christ!

In this climate, it was difficult to bring discipline, or to continue to live together in brotherly love. When Paul, now probably at Ephesus, heard what was going on, he was deeply distressed and quickly put pen to paper to spell out some principles.

From our 21st-century viewpoint, we tend to take in isolation each of the issues that Paul addressed in his letters, so that, for example, we read what he has to say about women in chapters 11 (headship) and 14 (women should remain silent) and resist what, from our cultural standpoint, we think he is saying, without appreciating that he was laying down principles in a multicultural setting. The letters to the church in Corinth (and elsewhere) must be taken in their entirety.

Paul did not say that women must not pray, prophesy or speak in public: he laid out guidelines for how this should be handled. In order to do this, he had to lay fresh foundations regarding how Christian men and women should view one another and conduct themselves.

Paul himself was raised as a Jew, in a strict tradition. This obviously must have influenced him in lots of ways. Yet he shows himself willing to rethink all sorts of aspects of behaviour in the light of the New Covenant. For example, he argues passionately against the old insistence on circumcision, the most fundamental Jewish rite. He vehemently denies its efficacy to give Jews special favour before God, affirming that salvation is only through faith in Jesus Christ. However, on his travels Paul circumcised

Timothy, a Greek, "because of the Jews who were in those parts" (Acts 16:3). This was not being inconsistent, for as he wrote in his first letter to the Corinthian church, "I have become all things to all men, so that I may by all means win some" (1 Corinthians 9:19–23). (This might be similar to a Western Christian woman wearing full covering in an Islamic nation, not because God requires her to, for "religious" reasons, but in order to honour Muslim neighbours and thus win a hearing.)

Let us see, therefore, that if Paul was prepared to put aside that most Jewish of rites, circumcision, surely he would also be radical in re-evaluating other important issues. One of these was the place and treatment of women. He himself had been nurtured in a deeply traditional Jewish environment, but when he begins to teach about this issue he does not appeal to Jewish tradition. He seeks to rediscover what God established at the very beginning, at creation. This, then, must underpin biblical teaching on Christian behaviour since it predates Jewish or Gentile thinking.

Doctrine precedes practise

Clearly, this young church at Corinth was a place of spiritual energy and vitality, with an emerging understanding of Christian behaviour which was only beginning to be formulated. All they had was the Holy Spirit and Paul – which was surely more than adequate! As time went by, eldership authority was recognized and order began to be established, but chaos kept breaking out. The problems which arose were life issues, and Paul tackled them, not by laying down rules, but by teaching the doctrines of human beings and sin, salvation, grace and justification, sanctification and the coming of the Holy Spirit. In view of these things, the early church drew conclusions on how Christians should live.

For example, in dealing with the sexual climate of the day and the way Christians should respond, Paul did not baldly state, "Thou shalt not ...", but taught the principle that the body is not meant for sexual immorality but for the Lord: "Your body is a temple of the Holy Spirit ... therefore glorify God in your body" (1 Corinthians 6:19–20). Thus by giving the believers a new and exciting perspective of the body, they would find motivation to use it as God's instrument for holy living, not for indiscriminately gratifying their own desires.

Out of this climate came a new and different perspective on women's identity. They were to be respected as God's creation and as members of the body of Christ, to be able to receive salvation and gifts of the Spirit, and to be protected and respected as mothers and sisters. They must also participate in disciplines and responsibilities: they were not to slander others, drink excessively, or be obsessed with frivolous things; they should order their houses and families well. It was recognized that women could be gifted to prophesy, teach, share the gospel, give materially, and serve in all sorts of capacities; in all these areas, operational guidelines were given.

In those days, a head-covering indicated modesty, respect and decorum. It was natural for a woman to cover her head in the company of men, and by so doing, she was showing her submissive attitude. It also indicated her bowing to the prevailing male authority. In some cultures today, this view would still obtain. In the West, a head-covering does not signify these things any more, although centuries ago it might have done.

When Terry and I first began to plant churches, we were zealous to be obedient in every respect, and for a few years deemed that women should wear a head-covering when publicly participating in a church meeting. It began to get complex, however, when we started to meet in home-groups. Should a woman now fetch a hat to wear in a small group that was meeting in her own sitting room, because she might feel the urge to pray? If she went to her cell-group and forgot to take a headscarf, should she be restricted from prophesying? I remember going to church one Sunday morning and placing my hat under my chair while I went to greet someone before the meeting began. When I came back, I found that the visiting preacher was sitting on my chair. I was too embarrassed to retrieve my hat from under the seat!

Experiences like these caused us to perceive that we were trying to force something that was not culturally relevant in our society. However, what had *not* changed was the principle which it was intended to illustrate, namely that a woman is under authority, that of her husband if she has one, and that of the church leaders. She need not indicate this by some material on her head, but she must demonstrate it by her humble attitude.

The "covering" of godly authority is also her protection in the ever-present area of spiritual warfare. There have been times when I have been engaged in fasting or deliverance and I know that I am standing on unassailable ground because of my position in Christ. But I also have authority because I am under authority, like the centurion who came to Jesus. As I acknowledge that I am in right relationship with my husband, and with those over me in God, I am standing on secure ground, covered, not naked and vulnerable. This may be an interpretation of the scripture which says we should have a symbol of authority on our heads "because of the angels" (1 Corinthians 11:10).

Thus, when Paul wrote to the Corinthians that "women are to keep silent in the churches" (1 Corinthians 14:34–35), it obviously could *not* have meant that a woman was forbidden to utter a word. The context here is about order in a church meeting. The previous verses are about giving place to one another in prophesying, and about weighing what is said: "For you can all prophesy one by one ... the spirits of prophets are subject to prophets" (1 Corinthians 14:31–32); in other words, people must apply self-control. The women must not chatter or interrupt the speaker when they do not understand what is going on. Evidently, there was so much freedom and so much excitement, that previously repressed women were breaking out of appropriate decorum and needed some boundaries.

Later, in writing to Timothy, Paul speaks with what sounds like restrictive severity to our modern ears (1 Timothy 2:9–15). But if we put ourselves in the place of a first-century church with all its attendant exuberance, freshness and joy of salvation, we begin to recognize the necessity for laying down some governing principles. He seems to be severe, for example, on the way women are to dress: "Women should adorn themselves in respectable apparel, with modesty and self-control, not with braided hair and gold or pearls or costly attire, but with what is proper for women who profess godliness – with good works" (1 Timothy 2:9–10 ESV). I don't think Paul is saying here that there is something inherently sinful about gold or pearls; rather, he is warning women not to be obsessed with fashions and jewels, but to give attention to those things which will gain an imperishable reward. This is timelessly relevant wisdom.

He continues: "Let a woman learn quietly with all submissiveness. I do not permit a woman to teach or exercise authority over a man ... For Adam was formed first, then Eve" (1 Timothy 2:11–13). This was not to do with inequality. As we have seen, women were able to receive salvation, forgiveness and grace on the same basis as men: the sacrificial life and death of Jesus. But now that men and women are in Christ, there is a restoration of what God intended at the beginning.

Recovery of Godly order

After the fall, when Eve disobeyed God, and Adam followed her, a dislocation in the relationship between men and women occurred. Adam was created first and given a mandate from God. Then Eve was created to help him implement it. She was to be his helper, but instead of helping him to do what God intended, she "helped" him to sin. Ever after, their relationship was topsy-turvy. Now, in Christ, what was lost begins to be recovered: "Adam" must stop abdicating responsibility and learn to lead "Eve" lovingly, and she must get out of his way and let him lead by respectfully acknowledging God's original ideal.

This is demonstrated in individual marriages (as

taught in Ephesians 5) and in church government. Women are given gifts of teaching, but they are not to assume a leadership position in the church, or indeed in their marriages. Thus, a woman must always be mindful that God has placed overseers in the house of God (variously called elders, presbyters, bishops, overseers) who are men. They are called to exercise the authority given to them by God. This, when exercised rightly and well, will bring women into security and freedom. Their teaching gifts can find expression in teaching other women, discipling them, in evangelistic contexts such as Alpha courses, and maybe in some counselling settings and seminars. Women are also fully encouraged to prophesy, speak in tongues, pray, and sing in a church meeting.

We can get so stuck on the apparent restrictions on women that we fail to see the purpose behind all this. It is not only for the benefit of the individual, or even only for orderly government in the church: it is the portrayal of a mystery. Ephesians 5 gives us the clue: right relationships between men and women declare something wonderful about God himself: "The husband is the head of the wife as Christ is the head of the church ... Husbands, love your wives, just as Christ loved the church ... each one of you also must love his wife as he loves himself, and the wife must respect her husband" (Ephesians 5:23, 25, 33 NIV). The key words here are "love" and "respect".

The world needs to see godly womanhood and godly manhood in pure, loving and respectful relationship. More commonplace is competition, rivalry, suspicion, scorn, abuse, and often anger and cruelty. When we work out our marriages and our gender relationships in the church with obedience, godly fear and love, we are making a statement about God: that his way of living is totally other than the prevailing worldview. The way we relate should make it easier for people who don't know God to see something of his character.

In Paul's day in Corinth, the church was doing the same thing: seeking to live in a way that was diametrically opposite to the surrounding pagan culture. In the darkness of a perverse and crooked world, they shone like stars (see Philippians 2:4). It takes no less courage for women today to go against the tide, to honour marriage, to respect their husbands, to submit to church leadership, and to regard raising their children as a serious occupation which takes their energies, their time and lots of faith.

Women and prophecy

We also need to encourage women in using the gift of prophecy. This gift can be a huge blessing in a church where there is a climate of encouragement, and where space is made for gifts to operate, and where it is properly overseen. In the church I come from, prophecies have historically played a significant part in our development, and also in matters of guidance.

Last week, as I write, I was helping an elder's family to move house. As they had prayed and sought God about where to live, a man (a regular church member) brought a prophecy, in a small meeting, which had an extraordinary amount of detail about the house they should be looking for. A few days later, the estate agent sent details of a house which incorporated these features. The elder went to see it and liked it immensely, but it was way above their price limit.

Unaware of all this, a young woman in their cell-group was walking around the neighbourhood where they wanted to live, praying. As she passed a certain house, she felt strongly that God indicated to her that this was the house he wanted the elder's family to live in. There was no board up outside to indicate that it was even for sale! She phoned the elder's wife and told her what she thought God was saying, not knowing it was the very house they had viewed! To cut a long story short, the elder and his family are now living in this house, having found God's amazing provision to be able to buy it. It was the prophetic words which gave them faith and courage to go for it.

Stories could be multiplied of prophetic words which have opened up new possibilities, or confirmed a proposed action, or encouraged us when our faith was flagging. It is just one of the powerful ways in which a woman can serve her church. (Philip the evangelist had four daughters who all prophesied.)

Boundries bring security

Many women feel perplexed about the teachings in 1 Corinthians 14:33–35 and in 1 Timothy 2:11–14, with their apparent restrictions placed on women. We should, however, view these teachings with faith, believing that God's ways are good. God does not want to confine and restrict women, or shut them up, but wants them to operate in security under the covering of an eldership whose members are compassionate and expansive, yet also clear about the boundaries they should use to protect and affirm the women in their flock.

A friend in our church furnished me with a helpful example of the importance of boundaries. His daughter's bedroom on the second floor had a balcony which was not fenced in, so he decided to place a railing around the area. Before it was in position, he realized that going out onto the balcony was dangerous. He was afraid to go near the edge in case he fell off and injured himself, so he hugged the house wall, keeping it close behind him, and did not venture out far. But once the new railing was in place, he had no fear in occupying the whole area and enjoying it. In the church, if there are no boundaries we can be unsure as to how far we can go; we can go beyond the proper limits and cause ourselves, and others, harm. Or we can stay safe and do nothing much out of fear. Boundaries define a spacious area to be profitably used and enjoyed.

A grasp of theology should underpin all our practice. We should never despise doctrine while seeking to understand how to conduct ourselves as individuals, and corporately as the body of Christ. For example, we can be quick to bring teaching on marriage, family life, behaviour in the workplace, and church governance, but if our teaching is not securely rooted in biblical doctrine, we shall become mere practitioners, and one person's opinion is as good as another's.

The eternal community of the Godhead

But the more we understand about God – the more he fills our vision with his beauty, grace, majesty and power – the more amazing our mandate appears: to be like him and to show him forth in the earth. As we dimly perceive that we are intended to reflect something of his glory, our *raison d'être* appears infinitely noble, and our status as human beings, far from being diminished, is elevated.

Right at the beginning of the world, this was implied in God's words: "Let Us make man in Our image"(Genesis 1:26). The Godhead wanted a people who would reflect the characteristics of the wonderful community of Father, Son and Holy Spirit. We know that God is holy, God is love, God is truth, God is power. God is also relational: his triune Person declares him to be, not isolated, but living in eternal community, and within that community there exists eternal order and mutual delight.

We are to reflect the Godhead in our social interaction. Authority and submission are principles which originated in God. Thus Peter can confidently write, "Submit yourselves for the Lord's sake to every ... authority" (1 Peter 2:13). By respecting and submitting to human institutions of authority, Christians demonstrate their obedience and likeness to the Godhead.

Our model for submission is Jesus' submission to the Father, which was total. In Isaiah 11:2–4 we read the messianic prophecy about how the Anointed One would operate: not by human wisdom or common sense, but by the direction of the Spirit, whose wisdom is of a different order. Jesus did not judge by what his senses told him; he waited to see what the Father was doing and joined in.

Jesus was submissive! But was he weak? Was he a doormat? Did he have to suspend all personality, all identity and become a nobody? No, he possessed incredible power.

A wonderful love relationship existed between the Father and Son. Jesus completely trusted the Father, and the Father completely trusted him. This is our pattern. Paul counsels, "Wives, submit to your husbands *as to the Lord*" (Ephesians 5:22 NIV, my emphasis). How can he say that? He enlarges on this point to the Corinthians: "I want you to realise that the head of every man is Christ, and the head of the woman is man, and *the head of Christ is God*" (1 Corinthians 11:3 NIV, my emphasis).

But was that only for the duration of the incarnation? There is plenty of evidence to show that Jesus always submitted to the Father in eternity past. For example, his coming to the earth was in obedience to the Father: the Father sent him. "God so loved the world that He *gave* His only begotten Son ... for God did not *send* the Son ... to judge the world" (John 3:16–17, my emphasis). Jesus himself said, "I have come down from heaven, not to do My own will, but the will of *Him who sent Me*"(John 6:38, my emphasis).

The writer to the Hebrews quotes a psalm: "It is written about me in the scroll – I have come to do your will, O God" (Hebrews 10:71; see Psalm 40:7–8).

Jesus not only submitted to the Father in eternity past, but will also do so in eternity future. This is evident from many scriptures which refer to this, for example, "Then comes the end, when He [Christ] hands over the kingdom to the God and Father ... When all things are subjected to Him, then the Son Himself also will be subjected to ... Him, so that God may be all in all"(1 Corinthians 15:24, 28).

Similarly, the Holy Spirit was sent by Jesus to the waiting church; he did not come on his own initiative.

His role is always to take the things of Christ and reveal them to us. He does not glorify himself, but it is always his delight to glorify Jesus. Yet the Spirit is one with Jesus, not inferior to him.

Why are we labouring this? Because it is important to show that the concepts of authority and submission are not just passing notions which had to be put into operation in a fallen world. Some would argue that, when men and women are saved, they are redeemed from this old way; their equality now demands that wives need no longer submit to husbands, and that it is all right for women to become elders in the church. But if we study the principle of authority and submission in the Bible, we find that it is eternally demonstrated in the Godhead; if we are to be true to our calling to show God forth in the world, then we must obey in this aspect too.

What about authority in the church? Why should women not be elders? Are we saying that women are not equal to men, that they are inferior? Again, as we take Jesus in relation to the Father and Spirit as our model, we must say "No". By submitting to the Father, Jesus was never saying he was inferior. He stated, "I and the Father are one" (John 19:30). Also, "The Father loves the Son, and shows Him all things that He Himself is doing. For just as the Father raises the dead and gives them life, even so the Son also gives life to whom He wishes" (John 5:20–21). It was because Jesus was submissive in every way that God entrusted him with mighty power.

There is a sublime love relationship in the Trinity; there is mutual trust and there is perfect equality. But there is also an eternal order: it will always be Father, Son and Holy Spirit, in that order. This does not detract from the worth of any of them.

This must be our model in the Christian community. We are called, not only to walk as Christ walked on earth, but to reflect something mighty and eternal in the very heart of the Trinity. No wonder our Enemy distorts our Christian lifestyle and robs it of value by lying to us that it is unnecessary, cruel and unjust! If we but meditate upon Father, Son and Spirit, we will see perfect harmony, power and love working together and it is this which inspires us with wonder, and with desire that we might reflect it in our marriages and relationships in the church.

Questions for group discussion

- **What kind of social or cultural problems might confront you in your church?**
- **What boundaries should women observe when exercising spiritual gifts?**
- **How does Scripture indicate that authority in the church should be exercised?**
- **How can the relationship of the Trinity help us to conduct human relationships?**

CHAPTER 10

A Dangerous Woman

I have this against you: you tolerate that woman Jezebel, who calls herself a prophetess. By her teaching she misleads my servants into sexual immorality and the eating of foods offered to idols. I have given her time to repent but she is unwilling.

REVELATION 2:20

Most of my knowledge of new churches is confined to Newfrontiers, a network of churches in the United Kingdom and in over 50 other nations. We call ourselves a family of churches, emphasizing that one of our core values is to build on warm, loving relationships rather than on institutional structures. This does not mean we are devoid of structure, and we try hard to understand and build on the patterns of leadership that appear in the narrative of Acts, and in the Pauline, Petrine and Johannine epistles. We believe in the church as God's agent for demonstrating the rule and reign of Christ, and church-planting as a major and effective tool of evangelism. If Christianity is going to impact the world, it will do it mainly through the church: the close, loving community where Jesus is the centre, the reason for our existence, and the One with energizing power to save us and hold us together.

Church-planting is therefore extremely important

to us, and we pour into it huge amounts of time, energy, people, money, resources and training. In our ranks we now have some very experienced church-planters.

It has been interesting to me to observe some of the difficulties and discouragements that often occur in planting a new church. Some of these are obvious: loneliness, financial pressures, settling a family in a new location, misunderstanding from existing churches in town, sometimes battling with a new language or culture when starting a work in a different country, the sense of bereavement when leaving close friends and family. All these can take their toll.

But there are also unforeseen pressures which can creep in. We can overlook the fact that as well as the normal "human" problems which routinely arise, we have an Enemy who does not want to see Jesus glorified and is implacably opposed to us building his church. Naturally, he exploits the usual "normal" problems, and a new leader can be so consumed with dealing with these that he can be unaware of nasty, poisonous spiritual problems worming their way in. Outward opposition is easy enough to spot, and can be expected; it is the insidious, well-camouflaged, subversive activities which can cause tremendous headaches, because they are often already well established and influential before they are exposed.

Over the years, we have been made aware of a weapon which is a bit like a stealth bomber. It is like a missile which enters undetected by spiritual radar screens, silently penetrating the fabric and often targeting the heart of the church. Eventually, pastors and elders realize they have to deal with it, and because it is difficult to define and wears a very effective disguise, grasping it is messy; it can explode with horrible fallout which can hang around for years.

What on earth are we talking about here? In Revelation 2 we have a graphic picture of a church in Thyatira, a city in Asia Minor, which was wrecked by a prophetess named Jezebel.

Perhaps Lydia, now a fervent new Christian, began to share the gospel with her friends and colleagues in Thyatira when she went back there on business trips. Some listened and also became Christians. When she returned to Philippi, Lydia told the church there about this new little group of Christians. The Philippian believers began to pray for them and eventually, when some of Paul's team were travelling in Galatia, they made contact, and a flourishing church emerged in Thyatira.

It was a beautiful church! It became renowned for its love and faith, its good deeds, and its perseverance under extreme persecution. It was a glorious, model church, full of happy believers, rejoicing in their salvation, reaching out to people in all walks of life, and ministering to the poor. In spite of the opposition which inevitably arose in that pagan city, they remained faithful. John the apostle became a regular visitor from his home in Ephesus, and loved them.

Then on one visit, towards the end of his life, John was perturbed to notice some changes taking place. The worship was dominated by a woman called Jezebel. She was an imposing woman with a fluent tongue and a strong personality. As he mixed with the church members in Lydia's spacious atrium, he noticed how people deferred to Jezebel; even the elders seemed somewhat in awe of her.

John met with the church leadership and asked what was going on. They seemed dejected, lacking in their former vibrant joy. When pressed, they admitted that there had been no new converts for a while, though their works of service continued unabated. In fact, several new initiatives had been started, notably some teaching sessions by Jezebel herself. But what had happened to the old joy and spontaneity? John watched and listened. He saw how Jezebel drew to herself an adoring crowd of sycophantic, weak people. She moved around like a queen, accepting honour, commanding attention, bestowing smiles, giving opinions – and, all the while, subtly implying that the elders were dull and regressive and not very bright!

Some members, however, were genuinely excited by her presence, her initiatives and her teaching. Others were confused but unable to articulate why they were uneasy.

Horrified, John hastened to rebuke the elders for abdicating their responsibility, and for not dealing with this woman's growing power. They shook their heads wearily. "We tried," they said. "She calls herself a prophetess. The church became afraid: afraid of her, and afraid of what would happen if they contradicted her. Suppose what she said turned out to be from God after all?"

The people were confused, the elders were impotent; Jezebel reigned.

Soon afterwards, John was seized by the Roman authorities and exiled to the island of Patmos. As he was praying for the churches, and worshipping, he was overwhelmed by the Holy Spirit and received a vision. He was instructed to write to seven churches, one of which was Thyatira.

It was a mess. Jezebel was rampant. By her teaching, many had been led astray, having trodden down their consciences into a state of acquiescence. Some had even fallen into sexual sin, as her twisted theology seemed to justify adultery and lascivious acts. In his vision, John understood that the Lord Jesus still loved the church, and having patiently given time for Jezebel and her followers to repent, was not going to allow his people to be abused and violated any more. Jezebel would be judged and those who had sinned with her would also suffer.

The same spirit that motivated her still operates in churches today; it could be called a "jezebelic" spirit. The following is a fictional story, based on an amalgam of different experiences from several locations, to illustrate how this vicious intruder can infiltrate the heart of a church and do its deadly work.

The story of a new church

The church was about two years old. It had begun with a group of around 30 Christians who were eager to see something new established. These people had become rather dissatisfied with their experience of church so far and found they shared longings for a church where there was more freedom in worship and where gifts of the Holy Spirit were encouraged. They began to meet regularly for prayer.

After a few months, they camped together at a Bible week, which was fun, stimulating and informative. They decided to invite one of the leaders they had met there to come and advise them about the process of becoming a new church. Regular visits followed from a gifted teacher, who brought a young man with him whom he was discipling. The young man, Dave, became very attached to the embryonic church, and eventually, all agreed that he would become their first pastor. So he and his wife were sent out from their home church and joyously received by the new group.

For six months, they hardly dared call themselves a church. They got to know each other by meeting in their homes midweek, for meals and prayer and worship. Soon the group had grown too large to fit into anyone's lounge; it was time to think about hiring a bigger room, and meeting together on Sundays. One weekend in spring, the church was publicly launched as Riverside Church.

It was a happy, heady time. The church members revelled in the joy and freedom of worship, and the sense of being a loving community. Dave was an energetic leader and a gifted speaker. Numbers grew, as new people found their way to them and then brought friends to hear the gospel, who were subsequently saved.

One Sunday morning, among the visitors was an elegant lady who appeared to enjoy the meeting, and engaged in pleasant conversation with several people over coffee at the end. She came again the next week and actually prayed aloud during the worship time. This made a good impression, and many people thought, "Good. A potential new member with some maturity and gifting!" She was invited back to lunch by one of the families.

Isobel became a regular attender on Sundays, and was often at the prayer meeting too. She was always the first to congratulate the pastor on his sermon and tell him that she had been praying for him. She was quite vocal and often prophesied. She seemed to have a lot of spiritual knowledge, which she was very ready to share. Dave was slightly uneasy, but could not put his finger on any particular reason. He noticed that sometimes, after she prophesied, the worship floundered a bit: her prophecies tended to introduce a negative, introspective note, and it was difficult to bring people's focus back to worshipping Jesus.

On the fourth Sunday, he asked his wife on the way home, "What did you think about the gifts of the Spirit this morning?"

"I thought the tongue and interpretation were wonderful!" she enthused. "But I wasn't sure about Isobel's prophecy."

"Oh? Why?" asked Dave.

Meg was cautious. She found it difficult to sort out her feelings about Isobel. She instinctively recoiled from her, and felt strangely intimidated by her "spirituality" and dominating personality. She thought that the prophecies she gave were not strong in content, but gained credibility by the forceful way in which they were expressed. But articulating criticism made her feel guilty. She didn't like Isobel's growing popularity, but to mention it sounded jealous and churlish. *Oh dear,* thought Meg, *I'm obviously the one at fault. I have a bad attitude. I must be more loving!*

Aloud she said, "It wasn't a bad prophecy, exactly, but it didn't really say very much, did it?" Then she added hastily, "But lots of people seemed to like it!"

Her husband was frowning thoughtfully. Eventually he said, "I think she's OK. I'm a bit nervous of her, but we don't want to do anything that might repress spiritual gifts. We need every person we can get, especially if they're keen and eager! I'll just keep an eye on her."

Later, at the prayer meeting, Meg noticed that Isobel greeted Dave effusively, and held his hand a long time while she enthused about his sermon. During the prayer time, she launched into a passionate utterance. Dave winced at one or two things she said, but managed to get the meeting back on track again. At the end, a little knot of people gathered around her. They tended to be among the more vulnerable and impressionable members of the church, without strong convictions of their own. Dave felt he should be glad that she was making friends, but was uneasy.

On Tuesday he spoke to his co-elders, asking for their opinion of her. They were divided. One was surprised, in fact slightly irritated, by what he felt was unnecessary caution.

"If we are going to encourage prophecy, we can't afford to be pernickety and suspicious!" he exclaimed.

Also present was a young man, Trevor, not yet an elder, whom Dave was discipling. Dave had detected potential leadership gifting in him, and had taken him under his wing. Trevor leaned forward now and volunteered, "We had some fun at the meeting in her house on Saturday!"

Dave jerked upright. "Her meeting?" he asked.

Trevor was embarrassed. "Yes, some of us met there for coffee. We had some discussion about gifts of the Spirit and, *uh*, well, dreams and visions and things." He saw the look on Dave's face and said defensively, "It wasn't really a meeting. She invited a few of us on her birthday, and well, it was such a great evening, we said, "Let's do this again!"

She's so lively and it's exciting, and it's great to hear about what's going on in some of the circles she's been in."

Dave felt rather helpless. He felt he had been put in a position of being outside an inner group. Questioning this development might seem like criticism of forward-looking people who were moving on in the Spirit, while he could appear stuck in old ways, unwilling to endorse brave new things. And it was none of his business who Isobel invited to her birthday party!

Nevertheless, it was high time to find out about these "circles" she had been in: what were they, and why was she not in them any more? It was time to probe a bit. Dave was reluctant to be too confrontational, so he decided to wait until she prophesied again: that would present an opportunity to speak to her in a measured way about her gifting.

But the next time he saw Isobel, she was so sweet to him that it was hard to respond by being negative. And when she prophesied, well, it wasn't brilliant, but it wasn't bad! He let it go.

Then one day, she went over the top. She broke out into prophecy, and it was fervent, emotional, compelling. It held allusions to angelic visions, and warned of terrible consequences if the church would not listen to "my servant who speaks to you". She sank trembling to her knees. The atmosphere was tense. Hurriedly, Dave announced the notices, and then launched into his sermon, but he felt strangely tongue-tied and wooden.

At the end of the service, he went straight to her. "Isobel, we have to talk," he said, leading her to his office.

Gently, he began to point out some of the features of her prophesying that he felt were inappropriate, and also some of the emphases that were doctrinally incorrect.

"Isobel, I believe you have a genuine gift of prophecy, but you need guidance in how to develop it. Prophecy is a powerful gift to build up the church, and it would be sad if it were misused!"

She looked up at him with eyes swimming in tears. For a moment, he thought she was going to humble herself and receive correction. Instead she spoke in a broken voice: "God gave me that word. I have been sent to warn the church! You don't understand."

"No, no," he replied, "*you* don't understand. I am the shepherd of these sheep and it is *my* responsibility to guard them. Gifts of the Spirit are given to edify, comfort and strengthen the flock, not to threaten and beat them up. Now, Isobel, as I said, I want to help you to use your gift to build up the church, not abuse it!"

The tears disappeared as she pushed back her chair and stood up.

"God speaks to me, and I must do what he says. I am sorry you will not receive the word I brought, but I still love you!" she announced tragically, and drawing back her shoulders, she turned and went to the door, injured but dignified.

On Saturday, the group in her house were shocked to hear that the pastor had rejected her prophecy, but were impressed that she had told him that she still loved him but must obey God first. How noble! How strong and how spiritual! One or two of the young women present secretly wished that they could be like that. But how disappointing that Dave was so opposed to her, so closed to her message, and so possessive of his position!

"Of course, he has always been against women," muttered one of them.

As everyone left, Isobel laid a detaining hand on Trevor's arm. "You know Dave so well. Has he always been like this?" she asked sadly. "I feel so rejected!"

Trevor mumbled something about how difficult it must be to lead a new church, and they were all so new to these things. Perhaps Isobel could try speaking to Meg?

Isobel laughed ironically. "Oh, I don't think so! She's not very spiritual, is she? And I get the feeling she doesn't like me. In fact, she may well be poisoning Dave against me."

Trevor felt frustrated with Dave and Meg. It was true: they were very unyielding in their opinions. Why couldn't they be more flexible? Poor Isobel was trying to help the church! She wasn't afraid to move into new, exciting territory. He patted her arm. "Don't worry about it," he said reassuringly, "I'll have a word with Dave."

He did, the next day. In fact, his "word" grew into an argument which left him confused and Dave depressed.

When Trevor arrived home, there was a message for him on his answer phone. It was Isobel: "Can I talk to you? I feel so depressed about Dave. I feel the atmosphere in the church is so repressive under his style of leadership." Trevor didn't tell his wife; he deleted the message and said there was a pastoral issue he had to deal with and went out.

They met in town and discussed the situation over coffee.

"Have you noticed?" Isobel asked. "No one dares

to prophesy any more. There is no freedom. Dave is so controlling!"

Then she told him about a dream she had had. Trevor was impressed. This woman certainly had discernment. He hugged her as they parted, promising that they would meet to pray about "the situation". He felt important, and drove back to the office wondering if she should give some teaching on her prophetic insights; they could be a dynamic duo!

When Dave asked casually about the Saturday meeting at Isobel's, Trevor was evasive: "Oh, yes. Good time of prayer!" He didn't tell him that Isobel had shared some fascinating insights and had opened up a rich seam of new thinking about the use of the body.

"Did you know that Isobel has had cancer?" he mentioned to Dave a few days later.

"No!" said Dave, shocked. He immediately felt guilty for his attitude to Isobel. The poor woman!

Trevor saw that he had softened and pressed his advantage. "You know, she has a lot of things she could teach us which she learned from her illness. She really battled with it and beat it."

Dave looked at him curiously. "She said that? She beat it?"

"Yes. She believes that God gave her complete mastery over her body, and she's now in control in a new way. It's only a temporary dwelling; it has no permanent significance, after all. She says that, as the body has no long-term value, it isn't really as important as you might think."

Alarm bells were ringing in Dave's head. "Trevor, that sounds very muddled. Our bodies are the temple of the

Holy Spirit, and our aim is to live in such a way that we glorify God by the way we use them."

"Well, yes, she referred to those scriptures ... It's OK – she's not daft, you know!" Trevor replied, nettled.

At the next elders' meeting, Dave voiced his concern. He recapped recent history: Isobel had turned up, seemed a lovely, mature Christian, had taken part, and made friends. But the prophecies she gave were increasingly disturbing, the friends she made were naïve and unstable and seemed to be looking to her for guidance, and she had started a meeting (without clearing it with the elders) at which she was bringing questionable teaching. Last, but not least, she was not disposed to receive correction.

The other two elders looked serious. But Trevor, who had been asked to attend, countered by saying that each of Dave's points could be seen in a different light. For example, people responded positively to her prophetic words, it was good to befriend others who were lonely and vulnerable, and surely you could invite people to your house for prayer without permission from the elders?

Dave leaned forward and focused on Trevor.

"Trevor, believe me, I hear what you're saying. But we've given her lots of freedom – too much, I think. We must be in agreement. Have you noticed how this issue is beginning to dominate our agenda – in fact, the life of the church? We're being deflected from our mandate to preach the gospel, shepherd the flock and grow the church. Trevor, you're being unduly influenced by Isobel. Be careful! I don't think you should be so close to her. Don't go to her house any more." Turning to the others, he said, "I think we must see her together."

Trevor left as they were arranging a date.

As Trevor parked outside his house, he was startled by someone walking up to him in the dark. It was Isobel!

"How was the meeting?" she breathed. "I just had to come and find out!"

Trevor grunted. "He told me not to come to your house any more. He says you're a bad influence."

She sucked in her breath sharply. "*Wow!* How can he dictate who should come to my home? He really is becoming quite tyrannical!"

Trevor wouldn't have put it as baldly as that, but he was angry with Dave and in a mood to be critical.

Isobel said softly, "Do *you* think I'm a bad influence?"

"Isobel! Of course I don't! I think you're wonderful – you're so brave. After all you've been through with cancer and everything, you just want to bless us with the things you've learned ... I wish Dave would just listen to you. It's all so confusing."

"You really are sweet," she sighed. "If only other people were like you, this church would be so different. You're not overbearing and egotistical. And you know that the things I've shared are all real. It's unfair that you should be made to feel bad for being my friend."

It began to rain. It was late and Trevor's wife was in bed by now. But he couldn't let Isobel walk home on her own and get soaked. "I'll take you home," he said, and opened the car door.

When they reached her house, she did not immediately get out. She put her hand on his knee. "Thank you so much," she breathed. The lamplight fell on her upturned face, and suddenly he was kissing her.

He drew back guiltily, breathing hard.

"It's all right," she whispered. "It's OK. It's only our bodies. We are in command of them. Surely we can express affection; we're mature enough to know when to stop."

He knew she was wrong, but he was already way out of control, completely ensnared, and he willingly allowed her to reel him in like a hooked fish. He shut his ears to his already weakened conscience. *After all, I'm free!* he told himself.

Two weeks later, Dave put down the phone with a shaking hand, his face white. A sobbing woman, Trevor's wife, had poured out a sordid story. Trevor and Isobel had been seen together, hand in hand in the park. When his wife demanded to know what was going on, he had flown into a rage, and announced he was leaving her for Isobel.

Dave held his head in his hands and wept: wept for a broken marriage, a promising ministry ended before it ever got going, a beautiful church spoiled. He wept in remorse for his own lack of discernment, his indecisiveness and procrastination, and his lack of strength and wisdom as a leader.

Eventually, it transpired that Isobel had already been put out of fellowship in a church in another town. She was known to be dominating, manipulative, and adept at ensnaring naïve people into immoral situations, justifying her behaviour with seemingly spiritual jargon.

***

Yes, this is a story, and one which some might regard as lurid, unnecessary and scaremongering. Others might recognize more than a few elements in it that are familiar, because they have witnessed something similar.

What makes a church particularly vulnerable to being invaded by a jezebelic attack? In what climate does it flourish?

1. *Lack of clarity over leadership.* We need to be very clear that church leadership is not a matter of human achievement or public ability. Elders are men appointed to the task because it is evident that God has called them (see, for example, Titus 1:5). Elders must not take up this role with the attitude that it is a career move; a position that simply requires a certain standard of academic achievement, an aptitude for public speaking, and a desire to be held in high regard by a local congregation. If a man approaches leadership like that, he will be constantly functioning with an ear and an eye on what the people like, playing to the gallery, fearing to offend, keeping everyone happy. He will not be forthright, fearless, speaking with holy authority, yet humbly serving.

Likewise, people in the church will treat him as a man they have hired to do a job, not as one of the shepherds who have oversight of their lives. We are commanded to respect and obey those over us in God, not to dispute with them or argue.

Nor must a woman be duped into thinking that church leadership is a matter of competition between men and women, and that she can fight her way into leadership. It is God who calls individuals, and it was his idea that the main leadership should be occupied by men. Men and women should live in harmony, respecting one another, the women accepting that ultimate leadership belongs to the man, but the man recognizing his responsibility to create a climate where women feel honoured, respected and free to use their gifting. The male headship should be releasing, not stifling.

Sometimes it is the leader himself who begins to manifest this controlling spirit. He abuses his position of trust by domineering behaviour, lack of trust, putting people down in public, belittling and intimidating others. The atmosphere in the church is very unsettled as no one knows quite what he will do next. He confides in no one, least of all his co-elders. He has considerable charm and uses it shamelessly to manipulate and scheme to get his way. Training others is not high on his agenda since he is not thinking of a successor or of anyone having gifting except himself. His desire is to have power and to stay on top of the heap.

2. *Weak pastoring*. This danger occurs when leaders hesitate to act decisively. They dislike confrontation (who doesn't?) and fear that if they attempt to bring some correction, they will appear unloving and unnecessarily offensive. In other words, they fear men rather than God and are abdicating their responsibility before God to guard the flock in their care. Sometimes, a leader can feel so threatened by a strong, controlling person in the congregation (but not realize that that is what he is combating) that he becomes physically weak and unwell, and feels he is battling against an overwhelming sense of oppression. He can become unaccountably deeply discouraged and depressed, so that he is tempted to give up altogether.

3. *Ignorance of basic doctrine.* Where a church is not well taught and grounded in truth, the people are easily swayed by plausible fads and new ideas. Systematic biblical teaching is vital for a healthy flock. They must feed well, and often, on biblical pasture, so that they know the doctrinal basis of their salvation, and why they need a Saviour. They must be strong in the grace of God and not be swayed by high-sounding, legalistic practices. They must be clear about their identity in Christ, and the authority that is theirs in him. They must be filled with the Spirit, walking in godliness, and bearing fruit for God. If they do not know that they are justified, they will become prey to attempts to earn forgiveness by human effort. If they are not clear about grace, they will indulge in licence or be bound by law. If they are not seeking first the kingdom of God, they will be open to all sorts of weird ideas and fanciful interpretations of Scripture.

4. *Unhealthy relationships* springing up among those who are lonely and vulnerable. This is where a good pastoral structure is helpful, to make sure everyone is plugged in somewhere, has access to a strong compassionate leader and is in a place where he or she can develop good friendships.

5. *Lack of spiritual discernment.* It is so important that we pray for and cultivate the gifts of the Spirit in our churches. True discerning of spirits is not about developing a habit of suspicion, looking askance at anyone who has the audacity to speak up! It is a learned ability to keep an ear open to the Holy Spirit so that he can bring an awareness of any interloper attempting to worm his or her way

into the fabric of the church. The Enemy uses all sorts of disguises to confuse the saints, divert their energies and spoil their relationships.

6. *Being swayed by emotion rather than knowledge.* All too often, someone who is inclined to seek power will not do so by obvious means, but will get people on his or her side by means of sad, pathetic stories, or by accusing a leader of treating them badly, arousing sympathy for the victim and anger against the figure they want to discredit. Clear scriptural guidelines exist for dealing with disputes and complaints (2 Timothy 2:25–26; 1 Thessalonians 5:12–15).

7. *Ignorance of spiritual warfare.* A congregation needs to be on the alert against the wiles of the Devil, to be armed and able to stand firm in the evil day (Ephesians 6). In our first church, a man began to attend who was sweetness itself to Terry and me. To our amazement, we discovered that behind our backs he was slandering Terry and gaining a following, especially among vulnerable women who were single or unhappily married. He was quite unscrupulous. Terry warned him twice, but when he consistently refused to acknowledge his guilt, it was Terry's painful duty to ask him to leave, which he did, but not without angry protest!

8. *Lack of respect between the sexes.* The prevailing spirit of the age is to foster lack of respect between the sexes, to blur the boundaries, to promote competitiveness, and to be in contempt of issues of submission to authority. We

live in an era when men are being belittled, and women are rising in rebellion. This provides a receptive climate for jezebelic seeds to flourish.

Jezebel is powerful, but not all-powerful, as we shall see!

Questions for group discussion

- **What other dangers can affect newly planted churches?**
- **What is the difference between a "strong" Christian woman and one with "jezebelic" tendencies?**
- **Are there times when it is right for a woman to challenge church authority? If so, when and how?**
- **How should a woman behave towards a church leader?**

CHAPTER 11

Jezebel

1 Kings 16:29–33; 1 Kings 21

Jezebel was the daughter of Ethbaal, king of Tyre, whose national god was Ba'al Melquart, a fertility god. Worship of this deity involved prostitution and sensual acts in his temple. Bronze statues were made of him with his forearms held in a forward position; fires were lit below them, and then worshippers would place their little babies in those red-hot arms: human sacrifices given in order to obtain good harvests. This was the kind of vile religion that this woman introduced into Israel in the ninth century BC when she married the Israelite king, Ahab.

Over the previous 50 years, Israel had become increasingly backslidden and had all but lost its faith in the LORD. All the people, except 7,000 men, now worshipped at the shrines of Melquart, and of his female consort, Asherah. These 7,000 were so intimidated by Jezebel and her priests that they were in hiding. One of the prophets who had remained loyal to the God of Israel was Obadiah, who had a position in the court of the king. He secretly hid 100 of his prophet colleagues in two caves and kept them supplied with food and water at great risk to himself.

So at this time, the Israelites as a nation were rampantly forsaking the God of their ancestors and running after false gods. In the palace, Queen Jezebel flaunted herself, overruling her husband, King Ahab, who in her presence was weak and intimidated.

***

Next to the royal palace lay a vineyard, fruitful and beautiful, with its well-trained vines in long, orderly rows, golden in the late summer sun, the grapes beginning to ripen in purple bunches. Ahab looked out of his window and sighed enviously. How he appreciated the position of this vineyard: its southwesterly aspect, its gentle slope, and the fact that it was immediately next to the palace. It would be so convenient for growing fruit and vegetables for the king's table!

He discovered that it belonged to a man named Naboth. Glancing out of his window one day, King Ahab saw Naboth hoeing along the rows of vines. He went out and ambled casually into the vineyard. When Naboth saw him, he bowed respectfully. Ahab smiled and remarked on the pleasantness of the weather, and asked Naboth what he thought the prospects were for this year's harvest.

Naboth pulled a face. "It's been so dry, my lord," he said gloomily. "Then that recent torrential storm washed away a lot of the topsoil. This is usually good soil, and most years we do well, but look at this." He bent down and picked up a handful of earth, and crumbled it in his hands. "Just dust!" he said in disgust.

"So you don't expect to make much of a profit, then," the king remarked.

Naboth shook his head.

"Well, perhaps I can help you," said the king. "Give

the vineyard to me, and I'll get you a better one somewhere else."

Naboth frowned, and shook his head again. "Thank you, sir, but I am content. Things will pick up when the weather settles down."

"Come, come!" said Ahab testily. "I'll buy it. How much do you want for it?"

"My lord," replied Naboth uneasily, "it is not for sale. This vineyard has been in my family for generations; it is my inheritance. I can't sell it."

The king's face reddened with annoyance. He tried to argue with Naboth, and offered a lot of money. But the man stood his ground. Ahab stalked back to the palace in anger, leaving Naboth anxiously scratching his head. He bent over his hoe, disturbed and worried, his thoughts in a whirl. The king knew as well as he did that families did not give up land passed down through the generations. It was virtually a sacred trust!

King Ahab strode back into the palace, smarting with anger and humiliation. He bellowed at the servant who offered him lunch, pushed irritably past courtiers who were waiting for audiences, and marched to his room. Slamming the door, he flung himself on the bed, turned his face to the wall and sulked.

When Queen Jezebel came in to dinner that evening, her maid servant told her that the king was in a bad mood and had stayed in his room. Jezebel's eyes narrowed. She rose from the table and hastened to the bedchamber. Opening the door with a flourish, she strode into the darkening room and pulled the hangings back from the bed. Ahab, lying curled up with his back to her, did not present a very regal figure. Jezebel regarded him impatiently, hands on hips. "So! What's all this about?" she demanded.

Ahab turned round to face his wife. "Naboth's vineyard," he mumbled.

"What about it?" she snapped.

"I want it, and he won't let me have it!" he said petulantly.

"*What?*" she exclaimed.

"I offered him a good price, but he won't sell."

Jezebel exploded: "But you're the king! *Huh!* In my country, we wouldn't even ask – we'd just take it! Leave it to me, I'll deal with it."

She swept out of the room like an exasperated mother of an incompetent child. Ahab made no attempt to dissuade her. He was used to her taking charge; it was easier that way. He went down to dinner.

Jezebel was thoughtful during the meal. When it was over, she summoned her chamberlain and dictated a letter to him. It was terse and coldly factual. "Proclaim a fast. Make sure Naboth is seated in a prominent place. Find two worthless men who can be bribed to testify that he has cursed God and the king. Then take him out and stone him."

She produced the king's seal. "Make copies," she ordered, "and make sure all the elders and nobles in the city have one."

Ahab was lounging among the ferns in a shady spot a couple of days later, when he heard a distant noise of shouting. He wondered what the hubbub was, but decided against going to find out. The less he knew, the better it was!

Jezebel came looking for him. The expression on her

face reminded him of a cat who has got the cream. She smiled slyly as she came up to him, and stroked his cheek with her forefinger. "Guess what?" she purred. "Naboth is dead. Now, isn't that a surprise? You can go and take his vineyard now. Go on, it's all yours!"

Ahab looked at her in gleeful surprise. He jumped up without more ado, and asking no questions, he went quickly to the gate and out to the vineyard.

One more surprise awaited him. As he wandered gloatingly around his ill-gotten property, suddenly he came face to face with Elijah the prophet.

Gazing solemnly at the quaking king, Elijah declared, "Because you have sold yourself to do evil in the sight of the LORD, he is going to bring disaster upon you and your house!"[9]

***

We have all met people like Jezebel. They may not have gone to the extreme of committing murder to get their own way, but they display many other similarities. We need to make clear that, although Jezebel was a woman, the same spirit can drive a man.

First of all, she is an intimidating character. She dominates relationships, makes the decisions, and wants her own way. She contests the decisions of others, including, and especially, those of her husband if she is married.

---

9 The biblical narrator of the Old Testament version of this story ends with a postscript: "Surely there was no one like Ahab who sold himself to do evil in the sight of the LORD, because Jezebel his wife incited him. He acted very abominably in following idols" (1 Kings 21:25).

Secondly, she tends to despise her husband or any male in authority. What she wants is power. She feels threatened if she is not central, in the limelight, getting attention. She wants to be in control, hence her compulsion to be the decision-maker.

Thirdly, she is antagonistic to prophets, although she may well be quite prophetic herself. The prophetic voice is authoritative, but it can also expose her, so she has an uneasy relationship with prophets. Her own gift may be authentic, but will get diverted and twisted, often becoming negative and undermining, rather than having the positive effect of building others up. Jezebel hated Elijah; after the contest on Mount Carmel in which the priests of the Canaanite Baal were exposed and humiliated (see 1 Kings 18:20–39), she vowed to hunt Elijah down and kill him. Although Elijah had won a mighty victory, her threat got under his skin and he fled to the desert, where he sank into a depression. This is not unusual for those whom Jezebel targets. Pastors seeking to deal with a "jezebelic" type of person can feel strangely drained of energy, depressed, and even ready to give up altogether.

Fourthly, she is manipulative and manages to get her own way by devious means. People find it hard to withstand her and may agree to do things they would not choose to do, or do not want to do, but somehow they find themselves manoeuvred into doing them! She can be persuasive, and it is easier to go along with her than to oppose her. Thus, a husband will give in to her for the sake of peace and quiet, although given the choice, he would do something different. The trouble is that she despises a weak man, but if she is confronted by a strong man she will exert all her energies to beat him down.

In the story of Naboth, we see how Jezebel so intimidated those around her that when they received orders to accuse Naboth of blasphemy and then stone him, no one dared to object; they knew the accusation was false but just did what she commanded.

Now, as we have already indicated, this controlling spirit can drive a man or a woman. If it is a leading elder who has it, the spirit will wreck a church. His subconscious desire is to be in control. He will surround himself with "yes-men" who will do what he wants. Anyone who opposes him will be crushed: slandered, put down and subtly undermined, until he or she leaves or is forced to submit.

The leader may have a magnetic personality which he exerts to win friends and display his "spirituality". He may be an orator who holds a congregation spellbound, but at the same time his marriage is probably a shambles. His co-elders dither about, because he will not allow them real freedom to make decisions or express opinions. If an elder dares to put his head above the parapet, he is ridiculed, often publicly. The gullible and naïve are led astray, instead of being gently shepherded.

If the leader's wife is jezebelic, she may masquerade as a prophet. Her husband has given up opposing her; in fact, he may even be very confused himself, because she appears to have authority, and seems to be very spiritual. But she can be given to outbursts of anger if she is opposed; she is jealous of other men and women who have influence, and manages to convey doubt about their character or gifting. Her opinion alone is the "real" one; only her insight and discernment are apparently reliable. She can frighten people, men and women, with her withering remarks, and her anger is to be feared. Her husband is usually in too much awe of her to bring any correction. Although he is leader in name, in reality it is she who influences decisions. She may display an outward show of respect, but in fact she does not respect him as her head or the leading authority in the church; nevertheless she needs him to be a man in a position of authority, such as pastor or elder, so that she can rule through him, as Jezebel used Ahab's kingship to authorize her deeds (see 1 Kings 21).

If a jezebelic woman is not confronted or exposed, she will either turn the church into a cult where her word is law, or she will split the church. The discerning members will leave, while the naïve and vulnerable will be taken in: believing her to be spiritual, they will regard her as their "guru". She tends also to have an unhealthy interest in people's sex lives, and asks probing questions under the guise of "discipling".

If a church member is jezebelic, there can be all sorts of ramifications. She (or he) will appear to be very innocent and friendly. She will worm her way in, but after a while begin to insinuate that the pastor, or another leader, is not really very mature. Subtly, she puts him down, while to his face she is charm itself. She draws others around her who are undiscerning and vulnerable, and implies that she has real knowledge and experience, whereas the pastor is a bit pathetic. She prophesies but it does not bring life.

Somehow, she manages to sow suspicion without actually making outright accusations, so that a sense of confusion begins to cloud friendships and relationships. She flatters people to their face, especially the pastors, but undermines them behind their backs. Sometimes she uses her sexuality to win attention and get under the defences of the man she targets.

Lies and jealousy also form part of her armoury. A young woman dear to me was once beginning to date a young man. A girlfriend began to insinuate all sorts of bad things about the young man to the young woman. She was jealous of their budding relationship and tried to break it up by lies and criticism. Her barbs were poisonous, and the young woman became very confused and depressed. Eventually, we realized that she had been affected by the jezebelic spirit operating in the girlfriend. The young woman was set free, married the young man, and they are now ministering very fruitfully together.

Jezebel's counterpart is a figure like Ahab, who colludes with her because he does not have the strength to resist. Like Ahab, he abdicates his authority. He might not have been weak to begin with, but over time he loses self-respect and gives into her for the sake of a quiet life. She has beaten him down, and so he becomes less and less competent, and increasingly depressed and abject. Basically, he is afraid of her.

Jezebel saps the energy and diverts the focus of the godly authority in the church so that, instead of concentrating on building the church up, and preaching and evangelizing, the leaders become preoccupied with internal wrangles and trivial disputes. In Revelation 2 we see how a beautiful church was afraid to confront Jezebel, but in tolerating her, they became confused and uncertain. Hesitant to confront her, they lost their sharpness of discernment. Standards slipped until it was impossible to retrieve the situation, and they found themselves condoning wrong doctrine, which led to condoning sinful practices.

This persuasive woman in Revelation 2, who "call[ed] herself a prophetess", misled them not only into sexual immorality, but into "eating ... food offered to idols" (Revelation 2:20 NIV). What is that all about? It is to do with the suppression of conscience. In the early church there were many people who were converted from pagan backgrounds; for these people, it had been habitual to offer food to idols. This food was then sold in the public markets. A new Gentile Christian with a tender conscience would have been uneasy about perpetuating a practice he associated with his former non-Christian days, and would have wanted to keep away from such food. However, in the same congregation there would have been Jewish converts for whom such meat was simply meat, no more and no less, regardless of whether it had been in a pagan temple. They may have scoffed at their brothers' tender consciences and tried to persuade them that there was no harm in eating such meat. But if the brother was troubled about it, to eat such meat would defile his conscience.

Paul taught that it was not the actual eating of such meat that mattered, so much as educating the conscience. If a conscience is ignored and trodden down long enough, after a while that small, niggling voice falls on deaf ears, and eventually ceases to be heard altogether. The person is then in great danger of walking into gross sin, while telling himself or herself that it is harmless. Jezebel, the "prophetess" in Thyatira, had persuaded a lot of people, against their will, to indulge in acts (including sexual acts) which formerly they would have been shocked even to contemplate. In ridiculing their scruples, she shamed them into crossing boundaries. Now they were in confusion about who they were; they had lost their identity and self-respect; they had become weak and spineless.

This is how cults develop. A persuasive and magnetic leader manipulates people into positions where their own judgement is suspended and they bend to his wishes, which may be vile and destructive.

So how should we deal with a jezebelic spirit? Again, Revelation 2 gives us the answer. There are two elements: zero tolerance and repentance.

When a jezebelic spirit is exposed, it cannot be negotiated with. It is irrational. A situation arose in a newly planted church, where a woman began to attend and make friends. She quickly became friendly with the pastor and his wife, and with one or two other prominent couples. She name-dropped habitually, and let it be known that she was friendly with some well-known leaders.

But it wasn't long before she became very critical of the pastor to some women in the congregation, while protesting to his face that she loved him and his wife. The people to whom she voiced her criticisms became uneasy and confused. Eventually, she was confronted by the pastor and another leader. She became so angry that she swore and shouted. When they tried to nail down some of the things she had accused him of, she twisted their words, backtracked, or changed the subject. It was impossible to deal with her on a rational level, because her condition was rooted in a spiritual problem.

The trouble is that it is not always easy to identify the jezebelic spirit until damage has already been done; even then, trying to grasp it can be like trying to grab the soap in the shower: it simply slithers away. We have discovered that the best policy is to pray that God will reveal this spirit in his time and in his way. Terry and I once prayed earnestly for months about a situation, knowing that it was not yet "ripe" for exposure. When the time came, we didn't have to force the issue: the situation exploded! It was very painful and unpleasant, and the repercussions rippled on for years. A huge tangled web of fear, legalistic demands and practices, and arrogant behaviour all came to light, as bruised and injured people tried to adjust in the aftermath.

Often it is in the early days of a church, or a new leader, that the jezebelic spirit makes its challenge. It seems that the object is to take advantage at a vulnerable time. This spirit is an enemy that a leader has to confront and conquer with boldness and conviction, because if he does not, he is likely to become an "Ahab". His spiritual authority must be established so that the sheep are secure under his leadership. This is hard, because a new young leader naturally wants to be liked; he may well feel vulnerable and inexperienced, and does not want to appear brash and arrogant. Somehow, he must maintain respect towards the person manifesting the problem, while not giving way to the manipulative spirit which is battling for control. Sin must be confronted and there must be no compromise.

Jezebel is rooted in pride; therefore the antidote is repentance and humility. When a person comes to a realization that he or she is being compelled by a jezebelic spirit, that person is in a place of hope. It is not too late for the situation to be rectified. As with all sinful conditions, the first step towards change is to admit they are wrong, then to humble themselves and ask for forgiveness.

We underestimate how powerful repentance is. It completely pulls the rug out from under the Enemy's feet. It opens the repentant person up to receiving the love, mercy and forgiveness of God. It is the total opposite of obstinately standing one's ground, entrenched in pride, demanding one's rights, angrily protesting that everyone else is wrong. Repentance brings hidden things to the light. When a sinful attitude is confessed, sight begins to be restored, and twisted thinking gets straightened out.

Questions for group discussion

- **What were Ahab's responsibilities as king?**
- **What was his relationship like with Jezebel?**
- **"Live and let live" (or "Anything for a quiet life!") is an attitude that some husbands adopt. Why do they do this? Why is it damaging?**
- **How did Jezebel get her own way?**

CHAPTER 12

A Personal Story

Some years ago, I went through an unhappy and uncomfortable time. Terry and I had lived in the United States for two years and had now returned to Brighton, on the south coast of England. I felt unsettled and disoriented. I had been unaware that re-entry to my own country could present problems! I had braced myself for culture shock on first going to live in the USA, but it had not occurred to me that I might need to readjust on returning to England. Everything had changed; there was no longer an obvious slot for me to fill, and I felt marginalized and unfocused. In this unsettled state, I was a sitting target for the Enemy's fiery darts!

He did begin hurling darts, and I allowed them to get under my skin. I perceived offence where none was intended. Terry's role was ever-increasing; mine seemed to be dwindling. I resented the fulfilment and significance that he seemed to be enjoying, while I was stuck at home wondering what to do with myself. Previously, I had been very happy and busy, both in my home with my large family, and in my church where I was involved in teaching women, and also on the wider scene, speaking at larger gatherings, and in writing. Now, suddenly, all these avenues had diminished, in fact virtually disappeared.

Looking back, I sometimes wonder if what I was

experiencing was simply explained by the fact that I was menopausal, added to the effects of returning to England. These elements certainly contributed deeply to my sense of unhappiness. But with hindsight, I can also see that they themselves helped to create a ripe opportunity for something more sinister to emerge, something which had lain dormant for many years. While I was busily occupied with my family and church, and "watching and praying", I could suppress and subdue it. Now suddenly, it came roaring into the foreground.

I began to believe that the reason I was unhappy was that I was being marginalized because I was a woman. I had been invited to speak at a couple of large conferences in the USA and the Netherlands, where I shared platforms with powerful women from other movements. They had different views about women in leadership, and seemed unconcerned about certain scriptures that place restraints on women teaching men and having authority over them. We got on well, and this aggravated my sense of being unappreciated in my own sphere. I was confused because I knew I had teaching gifts, but was not in a context where my teaching gifts were being widely used at that time.

So I began to crusade within Newfrontiers for a change in the way women were perceived. However, this simply compounded my own sense of confusion, because I could not get past the straightforward clarity of Scripture; my arguments were based subjectively on feelings and pragmatism, rather than on humility and submission to the written word of God. My longsuffering husband could see the pain I was going through, but also understood that it was more to do with my warped perceptions than actual fact.

It is quite hard to write about those muddled days. I remember spending quite a lot of time weeping on my bedroom floor, feeling useless, angry and frustrated. Again, looking back now, I can see that instead of asking God to search my heart, and entertaining the possibility that I could be wrong, I was blaming others. Who was I blaming? No one in particular, but it boiled down to men in general; of course, the nearest man to me was my husband, so he got quite a lot of my anger dumped on him!

At this point, it may be helpful to pause and observe that this is a common strategy of the Devil, our Enemy. He feeds feelings of anger, frustration and hurt. He finds a ready listener in a vulnerable person, such as a menopausal woman whose hormones are jumbled. Often, under a cloud of depression, she finds herself vaguely targeting "the system", or some other indistinct group, as a reason for her feelings of hurt. This is so different from the action of the Holy Spirit who homes in with rapier sharpness on areas of sin, highlighting with simplicity and clarity where problems lie ... as we shall see.

Most of the time, I probably kept my confusion successfully concealed, but I knew that it was boiling away beneath the surface. I went to the doctor and received hormone replacement therapy (HRT) which soon dealt with the physical symptoms of the menopause and greatly helped me to restabilize emotionally. This was a huge blessing! I felt "normal" again, but was still subject to anger and frustration.

In January 1998, Terry and I went to India with John and Carol Arnott. John was unwell most of the time, but coped valiantly with a gruelling schedule. The couple were a delight to be with. On the last day, as John and Carol were preparing to leave, their suitcases standing by the door as we said our goodbyes, Carol suddenly swung round to me and looked me straight in the eye. "Wendy," she said, "God is going to deal with a stronghold in your life!" I was surprised, to say the least, and not disposed to take it very seriously. Stronghold? Me? A mature Christian woman? Not likely – I was already sorted!

Nevertheless, her words came back to me, and I did pray about them. I asked the Lord to reveal to me if there was an area in my life that needed his attention. A few days later, I was cooking in my kitchen and decided to listen to a ministry tape from the previous summer's Stoneleigh Bible Week. It was some teaching by David Devenish about spiritual warfare. About halfway through, he briefly spoke about the jezebelic spirit, describing its roots and characteristics, the havoc it can cause, and how to deal with it. It was not the main thrust of his message, but it was enough to transfix my attention.

It was one of the defining moments of my life. I felt as if a sword had been thrust into my heart, penetrating to the core of my being. Everything he said described my behaviour! I felt laid bare, spiritually. It was an exact experience of Hebrews 4:12 where we are told that the word of God is like a sharp, two-edged sword, piercing between the soul and the spirit, exposing our innermost thoughts and intentions.

Standing there in my kitchen, I felt totally undone. A flood of conviction swept over me, and I began to weep. What had I done? How much damage had I caused? How I had abused the grace of God! How willingly I had gone along with the Enemy's deceptions, and how my pride had trampled on God's loving hand! Suddenly, in the light of his word, everything was made clear. The Enemy had been baiting me with sinful thoughts and reactions all my life; there was an area in my heart to which I had never allowed the Holy Spirit access. It truly was a stronghold.

I repented in deep contrition, and felt as if a stone was removed from my heart. When Terry came home, I repented to him. There were a lot of people I had to repent to in the next few weeks. The sense of release that came to me was dizzying! I literally felt light-headed, and very sensitive to the Holy Spirit.

Gradually, over the coming weeks, I began to realize the extent of both my old bondage and also, now, my new freedom. I had not realized before how jealous I had been of other people's prominence. I had wanted to be known, to be seen, to have attention. I had not recognized how envious I was when someone else shone, especially in prophecy and gifts of the Spirit. I had sometimes been upset when others had encounters with the Holy Spirit. I thought somehow that I had earned the right to have them! I was resentful when other women were invited to speak at seminars and I wasn't. And I had also put people down, spoken derogatively, and dismissed others' gifting. I had been quick to perceive offence where none was intended, and had been bossy and dominating.

In fact, I began to understand that a large part of this "stronghold" was to do with control. I was actually very afraid to "let go", to acknowledge that someone else could legitimately be in charge. So, although I believed that wives must submit to husbands, and on my wedding day had vowed to obey Terry, I had always been aware of a resistance in me, a lack of trust, and a fear that if I really let him be the head, he would not be able to take the lead competently (in spite of his having led a church and a movement!).

One day, after God had revealed the stronghold to me, I was praying and I questioned the Lord about this. I asked, "How come I was vulnerable to harbouring this?" Instantly, two memories came clearly into my mind.

One was to do with a childhood friendship. Many years before, when I was a very small child, a girl latched on to me as her special friend. For several years we sat side by side at school, played at each other's houses, and were regarded as best friends. The trouble was, I didn't really like her, but was powerless to break free from the relationship. She was dominating and demanding, and I felt suffocated and manipulated by her. I despised myself for allowing her to make all the decisions, but if I ventured to initiate something, I was squashed.

In those days, all English children took an examination known as the "eleven plus", which would determine which type of secondary school they would go to. I passed this exam and duly went to the Maidstone Girls' Grammar school. Valerie, my "friend", failed to pass and so was designated to another school.

I remember feeling a huge sense of relief. My life would no longer be dominated by her! There and then, I vowed that I would never allow anyone to dominate me again. I would choose my friends, and not be pushed into any relationship I didn't want. When the memory of this came back into my mind, I saw that on that day I was establishing a protective area in my mind when I vowed I would never yield control to another person.

The second scenario was of my parents. When I pictured them together, my mother always seemed to be in the foreground, and my father a somewhat blurred figure in the background. The realization came that, although my parents were kind, loving Christian people, who provided me and my sisters with a secure, happy childhood (which is a priceless gift), it was my mother who made the decisions, who had the greater energy and drive in the marriage. She was really the kingpin around which the home revolved. I grew up with the feeling that she could not totally trust my father to get things done, that he was not competent or able to make decisions; if he did, she usually overturned them.

I took this attitude on board. Included in my belief system was the feeling that I could not completely trust my husband in running the home. This was deeply embedded, and although I vowed to obey him, I used to have a tight knot of tension inside, a sort of fear that if I truly let Terry lead, we would end up in trouble! Of course, as our marriage progressed, I learned that he was certainly well able to lead! But the knot inside remained. It was not rational; it was an instinctive reaction rooted in the subconscious sediment of wrong beliefs.

All these elements coincided with the menopause, which I discovered not only brings physical discomfort of various kinds, but feelings of insecurity, dejection and inadequacy, so I was "ripe" for the Enemy to exploit this period of my life.

In this way the Lord showed me that certain influences

in my life had provided rich soil for seeds of wrong thinking to grow in. Being saved and baptized in the Spirit had starved them, but they were dormant and ready to pop up if conditions were right!

The apostle Paul speaks of "strongholds", defining them as "speculations and every lofty thing raised up against the knowledge of God" (2 Corinthians 10:5). Before we come to Christ, as we develop as human beings, we encounter events, people and situations which cause us to form certain systems of thinking and belief. We receive impressions and form opinions based on things that happen to us and the environment we live in. We form strategies and defence mechanisms, put up walls, and develop all sorts of ways to deal with feelings and issues. Often we are not aware that we are doing this.

When we come to Christ, our spirits are instantly made alive and new. But he also begins the "renewing of [our] mind" (Romans 12:2). This includes straightening out our warped ways of thinking, and teaching us to think God's way. Some areas of our lives can be relatively simple and obvious to deal with and are quickly changed, but others have deeper roots. We can be convicted about an incident of sin, and ask for and receive forgiveness, but not realize that this is like lopping off a few leaves while the roots, way down below the surface, are still active. Eventually, the word of God comes like a rapier, striking deep into our hearts, exposing the twisted thinking which must then be brought under the Lord's control. He breaks the power of that tangled root system, enabling us to learn to think his way, as we submit to him.

The metaphor which Paul uses, that of a "stronghold",

implies an area of strong resistance, guarded and protected. It is a system of thinking that has become deeply part of us, but which is in opposition to God's ways of love and humility. If we are followers of Jesus and want to become like him, such belief systems have to be demolished. This can be a frightening prospect because it involves change in the deep core of our being, so when that area is touched upon, we often flinch away and resist; we may argue and squirm and insist that our way is right, when in fact it is sinful and wrong.

The stronghold is in fact an area which is not under the lordship of Christ: it is unsubmitted terrain, and therefore a place where the Enemy wants to retain a foothold.

Whenever a Christian has an area in her (or his) life which is in direct opposition to God, which she will not yield to God, which she persists in clinging to and will not allow the truth of God's word and the loving action of his Spirit to change, she is giving room to satanic influence; this then becomes increasingly controlling and dominating. To be honest, I certainly harboured an area of thinking which was demonic in origin and was a foothold for the Devil.

What sort of areas are we talking about? Rejection, fears, sexually immoral behaviour, addictions and obsessions can be demonic strongholds, stubbornly resisting change and seeking control. In fact, control is mainly what the person is desperate to maintain and fearful of losing. As the Holy Spirit works in a person's life, the hiding places of the Enemy get exposed to his blinding light and have to yield. Often, many areas of sin are dealt with at conversion; others are hidden for a while. Sometimes they have to be forcibly confronted. Mostly, they are starved out by application of God's truth and by his very presence (through the process of sanctification).

But the jezebelic stronghold tends to be very stubborn and very deeply embedded. It is also fostered by our society and education. It is prevalent in modern culture, which resists respect between the sexes. It stirs up hatred against men in women, and cultivates anger, contempt and pride.

So how can we get rid of it? Paul tells us that strongholds are pulled down by "taking every thought captive to ... Christ" (2 Corinthians 10:5). There must be repentance, a deliberate turning away from the old way of thinking; there must be a recognition of sin and a submission to Jesus, embracing his way. It is a case of dying to sin and humbling oneself to receive a new way of living.

Jesus can tear the stronghold down in an instant! But we have lived in it for so long that habits have grown, so there has to be an active determination and refusal to act any more in the old way, and to replace it with living by the truth. That is why we are told to "be transformed by the renewing of [our] minds" (Romans 12:2), filling them with revelation from God about what he has done and who he has made us to be.

That day, as I listened to the David Devenish tape, revelation pierced my heart. As I repented and received God's forgiveness for living in a sinful attitude for so long, I experienced the "washing of the word", and a wonderful peace descended. God's love overwhelmed me, and in the following days I became progressively aware that the old knots of resistance and tension had gone. I found I was truly and happily embracing Terry's leadership; I truly rejoiced when other people were successful, instead of being jealous; I no longer felt driven by the need to be prominent; a new sort of happiness invaded me, a sense of peace.

For a while, God seemed to use my testimony a lot, and many women were set free. I began to wonder if this was to become a focus of ministry.

One day, when I happened to be in Cape Town, South Africa, I was enjoying the presence of the Holy Spirit in a meeting, and he reminded me of a picture which had hung in the basement of our house in Columbia, Missouri. It appeared to be a simple drawing of David the shepherd, sitting by a stream on a boulder, playing on his harp and worshipping. But it was cleverly drawn because, if the viewer looked closely at the boulder, at the bushes nearby and at the hills in the distance, he or she could discern that David was sitting on the outline of a fallen giant. This skilful piece of artwork came clearly to my mind and God spoke to me: "Your giant has been slain. It is not to be your preoccupation; your preoccupation is to worship me. But sometimes you will discern the giant in the landscape. You will have authority to deal with it, then get back to worship."

Jesus must always be our magnificent obsession. We are not to be taken up with demons and strongholds. But at the same time, we must not be unaware of the Enemy's strategies. Let us take hold of the sound wisdom of James the apostle: "Submit therefore to God. Resist the devil and he will flee from you. Draw near to God and He will draw near to you" (James 4:7–8).

Questions for group discussion

- **Can you think of a time when God's word exposed a wrong attitude in your life?**
- **Do you think the Enemy of our souls exploits natural emotion? When do you think women are most vulnerable?**
- **Are there areas in your life that might be the result of childhood or family problems?**
- **If you had a "stronghold" in your life, how would you deal with it?**

CHAPTER 13

Two Influential Women

Now the serpent ... said to the woman, "... Has God said, 'You shall not eat from any tree in the garden'?" The woman said to the serpent, "From the fruit of the trees in the garden we may eat; but from the fruit of the tree which is in the middle of the garden, God has said, 'You shall not eat from it or touch it, or you will die.'" The serpent said to the woman, "You surely will not die! For God knows that in the day you eat from it your eyes will be opened, and you will be like God, knowing good and evil."

GENESIS 3:1–2

The angel said to her, "Do not be afraid, Mary; for you have found favor with God. And, behold, you will conceive in your womb and bear a son, and you shall name Him Jesus."

LUKE 1:30–31 (SEE ALSO LUKE 2:26–38)

There was a woman, totally innocent, utterly beautiful, lovely in her purity, happy in her partnership with her man. Together they explored their environment, each new day bringing fresh discoveries, surprises, knowledge.

They loved and delighted in each other, completely and unselfconsciously trustful of each other. Together they were strong; together they were a team. Together they were contented. Together with the Father, they were inseparable, inviolable, invincible.

The creature watched them daily. How did these two function? What was the secret of their joy? He hated their love, their purity, their happiness. Above all, he hated the fact that the Father of all things loved them so much, and that they loved him! He hated the favour he bestowed on them, that they were like him in so many ways. The way they loved each other was a reflection of the way the Father and Son and Spirit were so besotted with one another. He hated them all. He was excluded, outside, jealous of their relationship, their power and authority. He wanted to discredit these new beings, tear a hole in the enveloping veil of that innocence, trample on that clean purity with muddy footprints, separate them from that powerful friendship with the Father.

Day by day, he observed them, unseen, unsuspected, waiting for an opportunity to get between them, to weaken the partnership, to insert suspicion, to introduce mistrust, to play upon innocence, to besmirch it with doubt. He wanted to separate them from each other and from the Father. If he could succeed, he would have them for ever.

Adam had spent the morning with Eve, wandering among the trees, identifying the fruits and flowers. Bright orange fruits already hung on some of the branches, but many of the trees were covered with masses of dazzling white blossom. Adam stretched up and pulled a fruit from its branch, slit the thick skin and peeled it. He passed half to Eve and together they separated the segments, and bit into them. Juice ran down their chins and they laughed at each other, savouring the warm, fragrant taste with its hint of tartness.

They strolled contentedly among the thick vegetation, sampling the different fruits. Adam, mindful of the mandate upon him to tend and cultivate the garden, studied the trees, noting their differing bark, leaves and habits. Some were low and bushy, their fruits in clusters; others were tall with longer branches, the fruit pendulous and heavy. As they emerged from the trees, Eve was delighted to find bright red berries nestling in plants that were spread in the grass.

Each new day was full of the wonder of fresh discovery. The landscape was wildly beautiful, lush with rivers and streams, in which swam sleek and colourful fish. Birds, amazing in their variety of size, colour and song, flitted about; in the evening, animals came to drink at waterholes. The man and woman devoted whole days to examining different species and plants, watching, learning, marvelling. Today was a Fruit Day.

By midday, they were sleepy, full of fruit, hazy with sun, replete with exquisite scents and tastes. Hand in hand, they strolled to a grassy patch under an orange tree and lay down; they were soon asleep.

Eve awoke first and lay contentedly looking up into the waving branches of the tree above her. The leaves were rustling in a faint breeze, and she breathed in the fragrance of the white blossom. Idly, she watched the lacy patterns of leaves against the blue sky; her gaze gradually became fixed on some branches – she thought she saw something else move up there. She looked away, then back, and yes, there was definitely something: a face was staring down at her with lazy-lidded eyes. She sat up and stared more intently. The creature unfolded itself and gracefully descended. It was shining in the sunlight, a long-bodied creature with glossy scales. Eve smiled, intrigued, and then it surprised her by sliding off through the grass, turning to look at her, indicating that she should follow.

She hesitated, looking at Adam. He stirred in his sleep. "Adam," she said softly. "Adam." He opened his eyes, but shut them again, dazzled by the noonday sun. "Adam, what is this creature?" she asked. But he turned over and went back to sleep.

The creature appeared to be waiting for her. She hesitated because she had never done anything on her own before; but fear was unknown to her, so she followed it through the trees to a small enclosed space. Then, with a sharp intake of breath, she realized where she was, for in front of her was "the tree".

She regarded it curiously. She knew it was special, set apart from other trees, not just by location, but by command of the Father. There was something different about it, because he had said they must not eat any of its fruit. She knew that, because Adam had told her. She and Adam had stood here before, and he had carefully explained that when he was on his own, before she came to him, God had given a command that they must not eat from this tree. They had both looked at it and solemnly agreed that they would not eat the fruit of it, and then they had walked on. After all, there were plenty of other trees, and unlimited delights, waiting to be discovered!

Now she stood at the edge of the glade and stared at the tree. Of medium height and graceful shape, it was attractive, but not especially beautiful. The creature surprised her by gliding immediately to the centre of the glade and swiftly ascending the lower branches. She waited, vaguely aware that this was somehow bold and irreverent. Those hooded eyes bored into her, and she slowly stepped nearer to the tree.

An intoxicating aroma reached her. She breathed deeply and saw some bright, beautiful fruit hanging under the leaves. Her senses were aroused but she resolutely kept her hands behind her back. Then she was startled to hear the creature speak.

Softly, gently, he asked a question. "Has God said, 'You shall not eat from any tree in the garden'?"

She blinked. She had not heard any question relating to the Father before. What had the Father said? "We may eat fruit from any other trees, but not from this one," she stated clearly. "In fact, if we even touch it we shall die!" Why had she said that? The creature was touching it, in fact sitting right in it, and nothing seemed to be happening to him!

The creature smiled, a slow, intimate smile, insinuating that he was sharing a secret with her. "You will not die!" he stated emphatically. "God knows that if you eat from it, your eyes will be opened; you will become like him, knowing good and evil." He shifted his coils luxuriantly, but his eyes under their heavy lids were watching her intently.

As he moved, one of the golden fruits swung out near to Eve, and its rich, pungent aroma wafted out on the afternoon breeze. Oh, it smelled so good! The skin had a glistening sheen that beckoned her to touch, stroke, caress its velvety surface. Slowly, she brought her hand from behind her back and timidly touched it. Suddenly, she felt hungry and her mouth watered. The morning oranges seemed a long time ago! She looked up at the serpentine creature, so casually perched in the tree; yet there was a kind of breathless tension in the air, as if something momentous was about to happen. Those black eyes gazed back at her, compelling, silently persuasive.

She felt very simple, lacking in knowledge. This had not bothered her before, but now it perplexed her. It seemed important to be wise and confident, like this creature who was so coolly contradicting what the Father had said to Adam.

Thoughts crowded into her mind. So God hadn't told them everything! He didn't want their "eyes to be opened"; opened to what? What were they missing out on? He didn't want them to know this distinction between "good" and "evil"; he didn't want them to become "wise" like him.

I would like to be wise, Eve thought. *Why doesn't God want me to be smart? And why shouldn't I eat some of this fruit? Why, I've been eating fruit all morning! Probably Adam was being unnecessarily serious about the whole thing!*

Anyway, the fruit looked overpoweringly luscious – too good to miss. Emboldened, she stretched out her hand, pulled the golden orb toward her and twisted it off. Plunging her teeth into it, she savoured the exquisite taste.

Hearing a slight sound behind her, she whirled around and saw Adam staring at her as if in a stupor. How long he had been there, she did not know. Cramming the fruit into her mouth, she picked another, and holding it out, she advanced towards him, juice running down her chin and dripping onto her belly.

"You should taste this!" she said indistinctly, with her mouth full. "It's amazing!"

The smell was reaching Adam now, entrancing and seducing him. The fruit was beautiful, and the woman offering it was even more beautiful. His resolve weakened and died. As if in a dream, he took it and stuffed it into his mouth.

The taste was unspeakably delicious, and they gorged on it, until both stopped, a bitter aftertaste puckering their mouths. Startled, they looked at each other. Adam spat out some pulp. Eve, watching, was irritated. "Don't!" she said.

"Don't what?" demanded the man.

"Don't spit!"

"Don't tell me what to do!"

"I shall say what I like!"

"But I'm the leader!"

As the first quarrel proceeded, they barely noticed an ugly brown snake with a triumphant grin on its face slither off through the undergrowth.

Nothing appeared to have changed, yet everything was different. The harmony they had enjoyed was disrupted. The blissful happiness had become tinged with fretfulness, and they were bickering and negative with each other. The landscape, no longer bright and fresh to them, seemed to have dimmed. They began noticing things about each other that annoyed them, and both felt strangely vulnerable, as if they needed to cover themselves, so they made some ridiculous clothes out of large palm leaves.

For the first time, both were terrified of meeting with the Father. There was some kind of barrier between them and the Father, and also between themselves. Disobedience had resulted in guilt and fear. Trust was now replaced by suspicion; motives were no longer selfless but self-seeking. Love was tainted, so that instead of being disinterested, it was mixed with desire for self-gratification. Innocence truly had fled and in its place was a new knowledge. Certainly, their eyes were opened, but to things they didn't want to see.

Eve's action and Adam's inaction had led to a disruption in their relationship. Adam's leadership role was undermined, but Eve was now vulnerable to his harsh attempts to reclaim it. She had acted independently and it had upset the divine balance. He had let her sin and then joined in, and it had robbed him of his responsibility. The consequences would follow them for centuries: dislocated relationships between the sexes, to say nothing of pain, grief, cruelty, disease and death. They and their descendants would be dominated by the Serpent until Someone could come who would be able to reverse the damage.

But that would require another woman.

And God said to the Serpent, "I will put enmity between you and the woman, and between your seed and her seed; he shall bruise you on the head, and you shall bruise him on the heel" (Genesis 3:15).

***

There was another woman, young – a girl really – preparing for her wedding.

She hummed happily as she took up her sewing. Dusk was falling, and realizing that she could no longer see clearly to thread her needle, she rose and lit the oil lamp. Shadows played around the room in its flickering light and she bent closely over her work to set the stitches in the embroidery. She wondered what Joseph, her fiancé, would think when he saw her wearing this beautiful robe. Life was sweet, she thought. She was going to marry a kind man, who loved her: a skilful carpenter, respected for his character as well as his excellent work. They would establish their home here in the village where they had both grown up and where everyone knew them, and have a family and be happy! *That's all I want*, she thought contentedly.

She thought she heard a footstep outside the door and lifted her head; at the same time, the little room seemed less dark. A brightness seemed to engulf the lamplight, and bemusedly she became aware that someone had come in. She thought it was a man, but she could not see him clearly. Then he spoke puzzling words.

"Greetings, Mary! You are highly favoured. God is with you and you are to be a very blessed woman."

Highly favoured – what did he mean? Why was she being singled out like this? She was troubled.

"Do not be afraid, Mary. God has set his favour on you. You will conceive and have a baby boy and shall call his name Jesus. He will be great, the Son of the Highest, and the Lord will give him the throne of his father David. Of his kingdom there will be no end."

By now, Mary had identified the messenger as an angel. His voice was full of joyful excitement, for he was delivering a message that was pivotal to the history of humankind. Jesus was coming, the long-awaited Saviour, and the rule and reign of God would be established by him. What news! What a prospect! The angelic messenger, who had just come from the very throne room of heaven, was suffused with the wonder and glory of it.

But Mary was not excited; she was trembling with fear and inadequacy. How could she do this? She was a virgin; her body was incapable of obeying. She heard Gabriel, but her thoughts were on her own natural limitations. She was young and inexperienced.

"How can this be?" she asked. "I am a virgin."

She received a straightforward answer. "The Holy Spirit will come upon you, and the power of the Most High will overshadow you. So the holy one to be born will be called the Son of God."

So God was calling her to a momentous task, but he would enable her to fulfil it. The Holy Spirit would empower her to carry and bring forth the life of the Son of God! In awe, she contemplated this. It would be the unfolding of ancient prophecy, a miracle.

The angel added some news: "Your cousin Elizabeth is going to have a son in her old age. She who was understood to be barren is in her sixth month of pregnancy. For nothing is impossible with God!"

Mary's eyes filled with delighted wonder at the idea of dear old Elizabeth at last getting her heart's desire! If Elizabeth was not too old to have a baby, then she herself was not too young to embark on this momentous, perilous journey. She was called by God for a huge task: it was risky, inconvenient, maybe dangerous. But it was not her idea: she had no doubt that this had all been planned by God. *God!*

She had the opportunity to withdraw, swayed by fear of inadequacy, of pain, of damage to her reputation, and by reluctance to abandon her own desires and plans.

Or she had the choice to embrace the Father's plan: the huge privilege of giving birth to the Saviour of the world. The angel waited respectfully as the young woman considered.

Her answer was humble and uncomplicated. "I am the Lord's servant. May it be to me as you have said."

Gabriel left, satisfied.

***

Two interviews with two women. The first woman, pure and pristine, was confronted by a being who beguiled her through her senses: the fruit was beautiful, luscious and fragrant! Then he exposed her own lack of self-awareness, insinuating that she was ignorant and stupid: "God knows that when you eat it, your eyes will be opened." Next he cast doubt on the integrity of God the Father, suggesting, basically, that his prohibition was not based on love but on self-protection, as if God were saying: "Keep her blind, keep her ignorant, keep her stupid and simple! Don't let her become *like us*!"

The sad thing was that she and the man had both been lovingly created in God's image: they were already like him! God actually wanted them to reflect him. They were like him in love, in relationship, in purity, in joy. But the Serpent implied that there was something that

God was withholding, not out of love for her, but out of tyrannical pride and power.

In fact, the Serpent was imposing on the woman the very thing that he himself had lusted after and for which he had been hurled out of God's presence. He had aspired to "be like God". Centuries later, Isaiah would articulate what is thought to be revelation concerning the Devil (who had once been a cherub called Lucifer), as he prophesied,

> *You said in your heart,*
> *"I will ascend to heaven;*
> *I will raise my throne*
> *above the stars of God …*
> *I will make myself like the Most High."*
> *But you are brought down to the grave,*
> *to the depths of the pit.*
>
> ISAIAH 14:12–15 (SEE ALSO EZEKIEL 28:12–19)

The Serpent lusted for power.

Eve's Enemy employed some very effective tactics to undermine her determination to follow God. His message to her was, "Think about yourself! You would be better off doing your own thing. You could be great: wise, able to make decisions based on what you see, smell, taste; you could understand important issues like good and evil if you were independent of God." He promised life, but gave death.

What the Serpent successfully tempted Eve to do was to act independently, thereby bringing about eternal separation from God. How different the result of the angel's interview with Mary, which was about reconciling human beings to God!

Mary was a woman like us, tainted with sin, but with desires to please God. She was not perfect, but God in his grace came to her with an invitation. Would she embrace his plan to bring forth life, while effectively laying down her own?

The Serpent made Eve look at herself and feel hard done by; the angel made Mary look at Jesus and be awed by him, while not minimizing the task before her. This was not an invitation to better herself, but to participate in God's redemption plan for the future of humankind. She understood, for she composed a song in which she recognized that God wants a humble heart, but that he delights to lift up the humble ("The Magnificat", Luke 1:46–55).

As Mary submitted herself to him, she learned a principle that stayed with her through her life. Let us see what happened as a crisis arose at a family gathering.

***

The wine had run out! Behind the scenes, there was panic. Now the wedding would always be remembered as "that wedding where they were mean with the wine". Embarrassing. Humiliating. And not true – there had simply been a miscalculation! Mary caught sight of the chief steward verbally tearing apart a hapless servant, waving his hands in the air, while other servants shuffled abjectly.

She sidled over and found out what was going on. Yes, it was a real dilemma! What could they do? She did what she always did when there was a problem: she went and found her son and told him. He always knew what to do!

Sure enough, he had a suggestion. The servants didn't like it. It sounded ridiculous, and they were not going to take it seriously, but Mary urged them, "Whatever he says to you, do it."

What? Fill up six water jars with water? How was that going to help? It would take ages too, and a lot of energy: each jar held 20 or 30 gallons! They were in deep trouble: things couldn't get much worse.

"Come on, do what he says!"

They felt stupid, pouring a lot of water into the jars when they should be working out how to get more wine. This activity seemed irrelevant, unnecessary, illogical.

But Mary was insistent: *"Do what he says!"* So they did.

Then her son said something even more ridiculous. "Draw out some water and take it to the steward."

The servants looked at each other in despair, but Mary's eyes were on them, and she nodded emphatically. Unhappily, the nearest servant drew out some water and carried it over to the steward. The steward saw the servant approaching and took the jug. He looked in it and sniffed suspiciously, then poured some of the contents into a goblet. "Where did this come from?" he demanded. He drank deeply. A look of wonder, then a smile passed over his face. "This is very good!" he exclaimed. "I don't know where you got it, but well done!" He hurried over to the bridegroom with a cupful, leaving the servant gazing into the jug with incredulous eyes.

Mary had found that obedience to God was not always comfortable, often unpopular, but always fruitful. More than anything in her life, she wanted to do his will.

***

Don't we all say this: "Yes, Lord, I will do your will"? But can it be his will if it embarrasses us, inconveniences us, and makes us look as if we have thrown away all reason, all ability to think logically? Does his will have to mean that we look stupid if we do it?

Actually, doing God's will means more than occasionally experiencing some loss of face; it means more than having to postpone something for a bit, or maybe giving away more money. Doing what God says usually means doing something we don't at first want to do. In fact, it doesn't just hurt a bit; it's fatal – fatal to our ideas, desires, plans and ambitions. But somehow he causes us to love doing his will; it becomes the very thing we want to do! Like Mary, we become his willing slave.

As we have seen, she had plans, and no doubt dreams and emotions that went with them. But Mary knew that so much more was at stake. This was much bigger than her affairs and feelings. It opened up unimaginable vistas which stretched into eternity! It was frightening, but it was wonderful.

She did it. She committed herself to do God's will. She became pregnant by the Holy Spirit and she had the baby in the most humble and uncomfortable of circumstances. She and Joseph lovingly raised the child, protected and nurtured him.

Then one day, she found herself standing in front of an awful tree. Nailed to it was her son, who had the choice to fight for his rights or drink the cup, to lose his life or save it. He gave it. In doing so, he became the bread of life for the world. If we eat of him, we truly begin to comprehend the knowledge of good and evil. And we find life, not death.

Eve has influenced every woman who came after her, and her influence continues, as we lust after things which God in his mercy has fenced off, and then live with the painful consequences. It has become inherent in human nature, ever since Adam and Eve, to aspire to be our own gods, to worship our own wisdom, to demand our own rights, come what may! This often involves flouting God's commands, overriding his principles for marriage, and treating men generally with a lack of respect, even with outright contempt! This is far from the harmony that first prevailed in the Garden of Eden.

Mary would not have thought of herself as an influential woman. She was simply getting on with life, caring for her family, doing what many women do. Later, she stood with the 120 believers in the upper room as the early church was inaugurated. She was filled with the Holy Spirit who came as a mighty, rushing wind and with tongues of fire. They touched her also as she prophesied and spoke in tongues, fully identified with Jesus' mission to spread his life to all who receive him. Did it cross her mind that she would become probably the most honoured, revered and venerated woman in history? Yet she herself prophesied, "Henceforth, all generations shall call me blessed" (Luke 1:48 KJV).

She was the opposite of Eve. Eve acted in her own interests; Mary acted in faith, forfeiting her own plans. Eve considered how she might be like God; Mary considered how she might serve God. Eve's action brought death and destruction; Mary's brought life and peace. Eve precipitated a curse; Mary opened a pathway to blessing.

Both were influential women.

Questions for group discussion

- **Why do you think Eve succumbed to the Devil's temptation?**
- **How did the relationship between her and Adam change?**
- **Has discovering the will of God ever changed your plans?**
- **Mary said, "Whatever he says to you, do." What do you think the implications of such a response might be in your life?**